About The Book

In *Finding Solitary Contentment* Victoria D. Schmidt reaches out to those who must adapt to life as single women after the loss of a spouse or longtime partner. She provides sound information and encouragement on such subjects as grieving, getting a handle on finances, establishing new social ties, self care and developing passions yet untapped. Her blend of personal and practical perspectives has much to offer those committed to moving forward on what is one of life's true devastations – the loss of one's significant other.

> \- John Dickerson, ED.D., private
> practice psychologist. Belvidere, NJ.

I read *Finding Solitary Contentment* from cover to cover then went back to review parts. The book is loaded with information, advice, gentle prodding and wisdom learned the hard way. Those of us who are on our own after life with a partner are the special audience for this guide, *"for the Widow, the Divorced, the Betrayed."* I appreciate the book's range of serious topics as well as eclectic background material, from the origins of Zumba to how to create an at-home space for meditation, to selecting a pet. Most of all I value the spirit of the text; it is for women, about women and from women. Author Victoria D. Schmidt is passionate … and determined … to help women grieve and move to renewal and new life options. Drawing from her own experience of loss, interviews with other women and current research, Schmidt opens doors to our possible futures and she is cheering for all to rise up and walk through. *Finding Solitary Contentment* is a tribute to women's capacity to support each other and create communities. Brava, Victoria!

> \- Lisa Hetfield, Associate Director,
> Institute For Women's Leadership,
> Rutgers, The State University of
> New Jersey, New Brunswick, NJ

An uplifting guide to singledom, *Finding Solitary Contentment,* provides a step-by-step approach on how to survive the shock and the grief that follows when one becomes suddenly single. Upbeat, engaging and enlightening, this book is practical, informative and educational with the author as your personal cheerleader and guide. With wisdom that transcends time, *Finding Soltary Contentment* is a discerning navigational tool for singles. This book is a must read for widows, divorcées and all solo women.

- Rosalyn A. Metzger, collaborative attorney/mediator and parenting coordinator. Pittstown, NJ.

*Finding Solitary Contentmen*t is **WONDERFUL!** What a joy to read a book that is positive and has a "to do" list for when you are alone, not sure what to do next. It's a "feel better" book and one that anyone can go to after a major loss.

I wish I had a book like this when I was going through my divorce, when my father was dying, when I became an empty nester, and when, on the same day, I retired, sold my house and moved away from family and best friends to a city where I knew no one. I'm glad that as my mother's cognitive impairment progresses, I will be able to turn to this guide and decide what to do next rather than grieve about my impending loss.

- Lynn Penland, retired Senior Attorney, U.S. Department of Justice, pursues her passion as a Certified Pilates Instructor. Tampa, FL

FINDING *Solitary* CONTENTMENT

Ways to Handle Grief
and Embrace a New Life

---

for the Widow
      the Divorced
           the Betrayed

by
Victoria D. Schmidt

To Beverly,
Thank you for your contribution to my book.
Victoria

Victoria D. Schmidt
July 18, 2013

Special note: Every effort has been made to verify the authenticity and accuracy of the information in this publication. However, the material is subject to updating and change. If you wish to contact any organization or individual in this book, it is wise to check the current contact information.

Initial Cover Art: Kathleen De Blasio
Final Cover Art and Graphic Design: Tomi Petrella
Editor: Linda Fowler

Published by Antigone Press, LLC

Contact Antigone Press, LLC through Victoria D. Schmidt at victoriadschmidt.com

Library of Congress Cataloguing-in-Publication Data
LCCN 2013900583

Schmidt, Victoria D.
        Finding Solitary Contentment
        Ways to Handle Grief and Embrace a New Life
        p.cm.
        ISBN 0-9860283-0-4

PRINTED IN THE UNITED STATES OF AMERICA

Dedication

I dedicate this book
to my husband Ralph.

*In the lotus there is
purity of body, voice, mind and spirit.
This exquisite flower radiates
beauty, innocence,
elegance, perfection, nobility and grace.*

Acknowledgements

It all began with Blair A. Pogue, the assistant rector of the Episcopal Church I joined in Virginia after my husband died. This compassionate, caring woman commended me on how I was handling my grief and suggested I share my strength with others who had lost their loving partners. I wasn't ready. Not then. Once I put the pressing matters of my loss behind me and accepted the path of my life alone, I launched my journey and created this book. I acknowledge that, in large part, Blair's encouragement inspired my passion to undertake and, after seven years, complete *My Positive Pursuit with a Purpose.*

I express my appreciation to the women I interviewed who graciously, and with an occasional tear, talked about their grief and struggles as they moved on to *Finding Solitary Contentment.* Throughout my book I include vignettes of these courageous, bereaved women ... whose names I have changed ... that reveal their trials to achieve renewal and embrace rewarding new lives.

There are scores of professionals, the experts in their fields and representatives of organizations and universities, who granted me permission to quote or reference them ... and validate the recommendations I make throughout my book. They are: author Anneli Rufus; columnists Mark Schnurman and Joan Lewis Smith; dressage trainer and judge, my daughter Lisa Schmidt; financial adviser, Jerry Lynch CFP; image maker, Sharon Kornstein; medical editor, Nancy Ferrari; physicians Dr. Alan Altman, Dr. Leslie Bauman, Dr. Herbert Benson, Dr. Joyce Brothers and Dr. Serge Kaftal; Pilates instructor Mary Alldian; surrogate Kevin Hoagland; therapists Suki Hanfling, Gina Ogden, Beverly Zagofsky and Donna Zahn; veterinarian Deborah Cronin,VMD; and yoga instructor Carolyn Geiger. The organizations and universities are: AARP, APMA, ASM, Mayo Clinic, Harvard Medical School, Harvard Mind and Body Institute and the University of Utah.

Then there are the patient souls who gave of their time and expertise to help me through or to contribute to the meticulous process of preparing the manuscript for publication. My special thanks to Kathleen De Blasio who not only was the initial cover artist for this book, she also introduced me to Linda Fowler, who edited my manuscript and to Tomi Petrella, my cover artist and graphic designer. I express my gratitude, as well, to my son-in-law, Wayne Rooks, for legal advice and Richard and Jane Altschuler, my longtime friends and publishing gurus, for their thoughtful guidance.

Among others I acknowledge are those who read my manuscript's final draft and prepared short reviews: Dominick L. Flarey, PhD, Executive Director of The American Academy of Grief Counseling (to whom I am grateful for also writing the moving Foreword for this book); John Dickerson, ED.D., private practice psychologist; Lisa Hetfield, Associate Director, Institute of Women's Leadership, Rutgers, The State University of New Jersey; Rosalyn A. Metzger, collaborative attorney/mediator/parenting coordinator and Lynn Penland, retired senior attorney, U.S. Justice Department, and Pilates instructor.

Externs Elizabeth Dante and Sara J. Takla ... students from my college, Douglass Residential College of Rutgers University ... showed amazingly mature insight as they offered their views and edited parts of an early version of my manuscript. I extend my thanks to them both.

My friend and tireless computer consultant, Salvatore Cirasa, deserves my appreciation and special recognition. He was always prompt to reply when I called for help to move my manuscript through technical problems and to transmit complex e-mails to scores of obliging experts.

I express my gratitude to all the dedicated individuals who have contributed to making *Finding Solitary Contentment* a viable resource for women who are seeking renewal and rewarding new lives after the loss of their significant other.

Thank you.

Foreword

Grief counseling and support are not new-found concepts. Unfortunatetly, it has only been in the past fifteen to twenty years that grief in our world has been taken seriously. In the past, society tended to shun grief, and to pretend we could not see it in our fellow human beings. Much of the grief was disenfranchised. Why? Simply because we are not comfortable interacting with those who are experiencing this difficult journey. We often do not know how to comfort the person in sorrow. We are often afraid we will say the wrong thing and cause greater pain. More importantly, those who grieved did not know how to act in society. Grief was hidden. It was a horrible experience and we needed to endure the journey in our own private way. Thankfully, this is not the case today.

Now, we encourage the outward expression of grief as the beginning of the road to greater transcendence of the pain. It is acceptable to grieve openly. It is acceptable to share grief with others, especially those we love. It is acceptable to stand up and say, "Yes, I am grieving and I need help." It is also acceptable to seek out self-help methodologies that will enable us to better understand our grief, to understand what "normal" grieving is and to find strength as we travel down a road that is often lonely and overwhelming.

In *Finding Solitary Contentment* Victoria D. Schmidt provides readers with an excellent self-help guide to coping effectively with our grief. Filled with personal experiences, this work allows us to understand that we are not alone. We begin to see that others grieve and that while each person's grief is a personal journey, there are also many shared experiences and feelings. Victoria's work reads like a conversation with a good friend. She willingly shares much of her own journey of grief. You will find that much of what she speaks about mirrors your own life and experiences with grief.

This work is plentiful with excellent and easy to apply self-help theories and principles that can readily be put into practice. It is truly a companion guide. You will find comfort in her personal trials as well as in the many ways of dealing more effectively with the emotions and challenges of losing a loved one. It will help you to confront your own feelings and emotions. It will allow you to assess your unique challenges. Primarily, it will show you that your grief is universal. We all take the journey at some points in our lives. Today, in our world, we do not have to grieve alone. There are more and more resources available and more acceptance of grief. This work is an excellent example of such resources and I am sure that readers will find this book of great value.

Let this volume be your companion through your journey of grief. By reading it and working with the recommendations and exercises you will come to know you are not alone. You will realize that grief is often the catalyst to create more self-strength and to reframe your life within its current realities. You will realize that there is light ahead and you will find yourself moving away from the darkness.

I wish all of the readers of this book a transcendent experience. Most importantly, I wish the readers a new awareness of the journey of grief and a heart-based willingness to help others who suffer its pain.

Dominick L. Flarey, Ph.D, FACHE
Executive Director
The American Academy of Grief
Counseling, Warren, Ohio

Introduction

"Solitude will renew you
and like the morning sunlight on flowers
touch you with peace."

– Susan Squellati Florence,
contemporary artist, author, poet

Losing the one you love, your significant other, is devastating ... you are now a widow, a divorcée, or you were betrayed. It may be that it was you who made the break. However it came about, you are *alone.* You have lost that special one who once was your rock, the person on whom you relied and with whom you shared so much. You are overwhelmed by the tasks you face that demand your attention. Another relationship is not even a glimmering thought in your mind.

The grief, pain, sadness and bewilderment that overcome you when you've lost the love of your life are difficult to bear and take time to set aside. I still shed tears for mine on occasion though he's been gone more than a decade. There are many ways to conquer or sidestep unhappy emotions ... for brief periods of time and longer.

The purpose of my book is to help you – *a woman who once was in a loving, secure union* – to achieve relative or complete *Contentment* while trying to retrieve a full, rewarding life. You may start with CHAPTER 1 and continue through to the end, scan the table of contents to locate the ones that have answers for you ... or you may skip to CHAPTER 14 to learn about one remote but enchanting option ... by joining the club of women who have chosen younger men as friends, lovers or companions.

A caveat: Though you will find solutions in my book
to help you through your grief and gain Contentment
you may still have a need to – and should –
reach out for professional help and counseling.

I do not suggest this book be read at one sitting. Instead, it should be used as a guide, a reference, to fill your needs. Go slowly. As you begin to find solace, savor each step as you progress toward your goal of *Fulfillment and Contentment.*

Among those I turned to after the death of my husband was Blair, a pastor of the Episcopal Church I had just joined. (As I took care of Ralph during his last weeks, I knew I should seek a spiritual haven.) Blair, a sensitive, intelligent, caring young woman, commended me on how I was handling my grief and urged me to share my strength with others. I was moved. I was moved to try. It took time, a long time, before I was ready ... and then I began.

My own experiences after decades of a happy, supportive marriage, hearing from women friends with similar trials and exploring scores of books, made me realize there is a need ... a need for one basic resource that offers places, organizations and people who give solace and guidance. My goal has been to consolidate in one single volume as much helpful information as I could find and present it in a compassionate, serious yet lighthearted style with occasional wit ... but by *no means* in a depressing or somber manner. We, who are alone, deserve to be uplifted!

I have chosen not to dwell too long on the suffocating side of shock, death, separation and grieving. There are volumes available handling these subjects in depth and with due understanding and sympathy. I reference some in this book. To garner as much as I could on how to escape the downside of being alone as well as the hopeful upsides, I searched libraries, the Internet, bookstores, everywhere. I conferred with professionals. I conducted interviews with widows, divorcées and others who were alone to learn how they cope and what brings them the most *Contentment.*

It has been, for me, a fascinating, rewarding journey!

You will find the book has two parts: *Part One* is designed to guide you through your period of grieving and to help you face your crisis with dignity. There are suggestions to help you achieve renewal and prepare you for the second. *Part Two* offers you scores of optional adventures to *Embrace Your New Life and Find Contentment.* Between the parts is *Passage,* an insightful, defining transition to help you assess where you are in your renewal.

Being alone, for most of us, is a shocking, new experience. We've spent our lives engaging in what is expected of us and respecting traditional mores. From infancy to young adulthood, our parents guide us (though some of us are left in the care of others), we go to school, we play ... we are loved and we are taught how to handle happiness and disappointments ... we go to college and/or get a job, get married and have our own children. We respond to their needs. We're involved in the community, the arts, watch the news and pursue hobbies and other interests. We're swept up in the demands, the pressures and stresses of everyday life never having, needing or taking time to contemplate how or why we are on the course we follow.

The lives of some of us, in our earlier years, are interrupted with upheavals ... accidents, loss of employment, illness, death of loved ones, divorce ... that violate this tranquil existence. However, most of us, fortunately, continue more or less happily with only an occasional disruption within a comfortable day-to-day routine.

Suddenly, often without warning, through the death of our spouse, divorce, neglect or betrayal ... we are *alone!* Some of us still have young children, others have those who are grown and have gone on to lead lives of their own. You are faced with stunning new challenges. Were you (or are you) prepared to take charge, handle the funeral arrangements, work with a divorce attorney, file the proper documents, take the reins of the family finances, face family and friends with courage and undertake a new, fulfilling life? Alone? A huge undertaking!

You may be alone
but you do not have to be lonely ... or lonesome!

I have assembled sections in my book that most of us who are without partners have the most need. For those of you who are unsure which path to take, where to turn or lack a grasp of self-image, I have included chapters to help you find yourself and realize where and how your greatest problems may be solved. On occasion, I repeat a particularly valuable suggestion in another chapter and in some cases I expand on it. For those who need additional information, I list publications, websites, organizations and individuals you can turn to.

Again, a caveat: Though you will find solutions in my book

*to help you through your grief and gain Solitary Contentment
you may still have a need to ... and should ... reach out
to a Grief Counselor or others for professional help .*

You will find information to help you explore people, ways and places you may not have considered or believed acceptable. Do you feel you are too old to find a new significant other? A man younger than you? How about a woman as a live-in companion ... or even as a lover?

Have you explored getting a job if you never held one ... or changing jobs to experience new people and a new environment? Or taking or adding a volunteer job that will give you a sense of gratification and contribution?

What about pulling up stakes and moving to another state ... another country? Not immediately but sometime in the future. How about Paris, Montana, Costa Rica, a Greek island or a small, friendly village in your own state? You may be surprised to learn of places that have a slower pace and will bring you a sense of peace. Planning and researching the area you focus on, can, in itself, be a happy distraction.

There are many more options throughout my book. You may explore them to help you find your path to *Fulfillment and Contentment* or *Contentment* with someone new who will bring you happiness.

Always remember, *it is time to take charge of your life!*

Best wishes,

Victoria D. Schmidt

Table of Contents

Part One
Renewal

1

Passage
Renewal to Adventures
(New Life Options)

111

Part Two
New Life Options – Adventures

115

APPENDIX

Part One

Renewal

CHAPTER 1

How Content Are You with Your Solitude?

*"When you get to the end of your rope,
tie a knot in it and hang on."*

— Eleanor Roosevelt, 1884-1962,
First Lady and UN Delegate

*E*ven if you are in the midst of a solid relationship, there are times you find yourself alone. However, without a partner or companion those times occur more often and for some of you, you flounder and find *no* moments of *Contentment* at all. The degrees of *Contentment* vary and you may need more or less help than you feel is necessary. Try this test and find out how to rate your *Contentment* when you have been left alone. The chapters that follow offer answers to most if not all of your needs.

Fill in the O for each statement on the next page under the category that fits you best or closely. Then take the totals on the following page to learn how you rank.

Rankings

5 points: That's me
4 points: That's me a little
3 points: That may be me
2 points: I'm not sure
1 point: That's not me at all

3

The Elements

	5	4	3	2	1
1. I grieve but not long or often	O	O	O	O	O
2 I'm happy in and with my home	O	O	O	O	O
3. I'm in good health	O	O	O	O	O
4. I visit my doctor and dentist regularly	O	O	O	O	O
5. I'm physically fit	O	O	O	O	O
6. I exercise	O	O	O	O	O
7. I'm acceptably attractive or more	O	O	O	O	O
8. I'm rarely depressed or stressed out	O	O	O	O	O
9. I don't worry often	O	O	O	O	O
10. My finances are in good order. I'm financially secure	O	O	O	O	O
11. I have an estate plan	O	O	O	O	O
12. My children (family) support me	O	O	O	O	O
13. I attend church or other spiritual meetings on occasion	O	O	O	O	O
14. I have a rewarding job and/or I do volunteer work	O	O	O	O	O
15. I travel from time to time	O	O	O	O	O
16. I have several friends	O	O	O	O	O
17. I have a very good friend I can rely on	O	O	O	O	O
18. I feel secure about my future	O	O	O	O	O
19. I know where to turn if I need help or guidance	O	O	O	O	O
20. I have a hobby (hobbies)	O	O	O	O	O
21. I make sure I escape and go to movies, concerts, theater, etc. from time to time	O	O	O	O	O

Line Totals ____ ____ ____ ____ ____

Final Total _____

Your rating based on total points:

90 -105 points:
You don't need much help/advice but read the book anyway.

70 - 89 points:
You're okay but you need to work on your weak elements.

40 - 69 points:
It will take a while but you'll make it.

1 - 39 points:
You have a long road ahead but if you set your sights high on achieving *Contentment* in your solitude, you will.

Regardless of how you rank in this "test" you may have more or less *Contentment* than your score indicates. The list is designed to acquaint you with the elements that contribute to your state of well-being. The chapters that follow offer ways and options that will help you improve your score and find greater *Contentment*.

CHAPTER 2

The First Hurdle:
the Shock and the Grief

*"Sometimes we need to be alone with our grief and
our memories. We just need to guard against making this
our only response for it's not healthy."*

— Evangelist Billy Graham

*Y*ou are alone because you lost the partner you loved and trusted. Your loved one is gone because he/she

died suddenly ... in an accident or of a heart attack
passed away after a long, lingering illness
left after a bitter/amicable divorce/separation
was neglectful or betrayed you

Whatever the cause, *you* are alone!

After several years of a happy marriage/relationship ... ten, twenty, thirty years, perhaps more ... you find yourself single again with a deep sense of loss and emptiness. You experience emotions you've never felt before. You may even have thought you were prepared for the shock and could handle it. But you can't!

You may have seen it happen to friends, acquaintances or relatives, or watched similar cases on *The Oprah Winfrey Show,* but you never imagined it would happen to you. But it has.

What do you feel?

Shock, fear, neglect, rejection, betrayal, guilt, anger, bewilderment, numbness, despair. Perhaps not all of these but at least a few and some with great intensity. Gratefully, most are temporary. You're entitled,

7

now, and to continue to have these emotions until with passing time, your inner strength takes hold and brings back your serenity.

Who suffers the most?

We all have pain and we are so consumed with our grief we are convinced that ours is the greatest. No doubt it is, to us. After having interviewed those who lost their significant others I found a silent undercurrent from those who were divorced or deserted (not the widowed). They have a deeper sense of rejection and betrayal. Not all, but many are more bitter, lose trust in others and delay or prolong closure. They have to work harder to achieve *Contentment*, but they, too, can succeed.

I lost my husband Ralph after being his caregiver for five long years as he declined very slowly, suffering from Parkinson's disease. He slipped away from me, little by little. He had been my rock.

Then, he was gone.

Only the death of a child is more devastating than the loss of a loving partner. Except for my daughter and her husband I have seen the rest of my close family pass away: both sets of my grandparents, my mother, my father, my sister, my brother, six uncles … and distant relatives and friends. Ralph was with me and helped me face these losses. But his leaving me has been the most heart-wrenching sorrow of all. And, of course, the loss of your lover has been yours.

Though our doctors told me Ralph was close to dying, they could not predict when. For the first days after his death I was in denial. I had so many details to attend to, there was little time to feel or acknowledge his passing. Suddenly, a week later, I went into shock. My strongest emotion was emptiness. I expected Ralph to walk into the kitchen as I was cooking or, I'd look out the window thinking I'd see him working in the garden he loved.

The loneliness weighed heavily.

About three months later, **Margery,** a college friend whom I'd not seen for sometime, came to visit. She had lost her husband suddenly of a heart attack several years earlier. As we reminisced about our happy times together as a foursome, I wanted to ask her how long the feelings of grief and loss would last. I tried, but I did not. I could not. I was afraid to hear what she would say.

Since then, I have realized that it is different for everyone, and may take longer than expected. But there are steps you can undertake to fill the void.

As years go by ... the times you may feel those emotions come less and less often. They do return ... and sometimes as strongly as the day of your loss ... but you can exchange them for positive memories. It is never easy but it can be done.

Before the times of grief grow fewer, there are hurdles that, first, should be overcome.

The Importance of Grieving

"Mourning the loss of someone you love is happiness compared with having to live with someone you hate."

– Jean de La Bruyère, 1645-1696,
French writer

Grieve!

Putting on an act of bravery and courage in public may be commendable, but among close friends and family a false front may be detrimental and delay and prolong the necessary process of grieving. However, grief shown in public sometimes is okay, too.

Grieving is like splashing your face with cold water. It wakens your senses to reality. It is an acceptance of loss and opens the path to healing.

It will help you overcome denial.

Cry!

Cry. Cry louder, *in private,* than you ever cried before. Shed tears ... let them flow like a rapid river that empties into the ocean. (Catch them in one of your love's large handkerchiefs.) If you are with others and the tears press behind your eyes, let them trickle down your cheeks. Your friends will understand and give you a hug.

Talk!

Friends and relatives will ask how they can help. Most feel awkward

9

and don't know what to say or do. Talk with them and pour out your heart. It is a release for you and a relief for them because they want to be there for you. It is comforting for both of you. Days after I was a widow, I started going to church again. During the coffee hour, a lovely blond woman in her late 60s approached me. She sensed my grief.

"I'm **Carolyn.** You've lost someone," she said quietly. "Yes, my husband," I replied, choking up at the kindness and understanding she expressed. Tears came, I could not hold them back. She told me that four years earlier she lost her husband to Parkinson's disease … just as Ralph had succumbed. We arranged to have lunch together where we talked and talked and talked some more. It was gratifying for me *and* for Carolyn.

Grieve more!

The sooner you accept the need to grieve, the sooner the pain and the hurt will subside and the sooner you will launch your new life and experience *Contentment.* You may not want a new life … you are in denial as many others who have lost their loves.

But your loved one *is* gone.

My good friend Ken, who was often there for me right after Ralph died, reminded me that I would be starting a new life. I did not understand what he was trying to tell me. I denied the truth again and again. I expected my life to continue in the same way I'd lived for decades with my husband. I wanted no change. I did not want to let go. As months passed, there were times the void left by Ralph's absence became overwhelming. I grieved but gradually I realized that, yes, I would have to fill that void. When the grieving became too painful, I tried to look forward to whatever the future would bring. The grieving helped me face reality. I was, indeed, about to start a new life, as much as I had been denying its inevitability. Denial is powerful *and* is best overcome.

Grieve as long as it takes.

The time of grieving and the other emotions that are brought about by death, divorce, separation or neglect are not the same for everyone and can last longer than expected. Further, there are reminders that bring back the pain once the original grieving has passed ... anniversaries, holidays, music, a letter, photographs. It happens. Just let the tears flow again if they must, they will again relieve the hurt. There are occasions when I am jarred by a reminder and revert. I want to hold onto the past. Then I forgive myself and return to reality for the past should not take over the present.

By permitting yourself to grieve and by setting aside denial you may avoid the floundering that allows your life to wander and take a course of its own ... not the one you would choose if your loved one were still with you.

Letting go of grief.

There comes a time when we must let go of our grief ... the deep pain and hurt ... not the healing memories. If your loss was through death, you need not feel guilt that you are betraying the one you lost by planning a future alone. Your love will continue and often grows stronger. If the loss were through divorce, neglect or betrayal, it is best to put that relationship behind you as soon as you can and move on. Remember Billy Graham's caveat that making grieving our only response is not healthy.

Letting go, after a period of grieving, will help you *take charge of your life.*

Handling Negative Emotions

Don't punish yourself!

Most negative emotions following the loss of a lover, such as fear, anger, depression, anxiety, stress, foreboding, horror and thoughts of suicide, are temporary and disappear in time or evolve into calmer thoughts and positive emotions. Punishing yourself and having guilt for experiencing them can be harmful and as counter-productive as rejecting the need for grieving. Continuing them will delay your path to *Contentment.*

Let them go!

Anger.

In a widows' discussion group I attended shortly after my loss, I was

11

taken aback to hear one widow, who lost her husband five years earlier, tell of her anger with him for leaving her without having explained their finances. Her anger persisted and hindered her search for the documents. Finally, after almost a year, with the help of a lawyer and an accountant, her problems were resolved. What surprised me most was that she still harbored the anger after so long a time. She may have been justified to have temporary anger because her husband was at fault, but she had not made any effort to find *Contentment* and her life was miserable and filled with tarnished memories.

Horror.

This emotion can be the most difficult to face and overcome. I'm having trouble now as I write about my experience with horror. Watching a loved one die or seeing him/her soon after death brings on uncontrollable feelings of grief ... *horror.*

I knew my husband Ralph was dying but when I received the call at one o'clock that June morning, I was unbelieving. Strangely, I shifted into automatic pilot. I threw on clothes, I can't recall which. I called the funeral home which had been alerted for some time. I summoned my household helper and together we drove to the nursing home. *I* drove. I would not have it otherwise. I was numb but in control. I could not utter a word. The calm at the facility was eerie. The hearse driver had already arrived. The male nurse was sympathetic. "You may go in," he whispered. "His mouth is open. I'm sorry, we could not close it." I had visited Ralph the afternoon before. Though subdued, he'd been alive. Now he was dead!

This vision often returns, even today. It takes effort but I push it out of my mind and make sure I evoke happy memories of the wonderful life we shared. I cannot let the negatives of the past take over the present.

Donna, twice a widow, lost one husband after a long illness and the second suddenly. She loved them both dearly, but in different ways. Her horror was twofold, and similar. Both men died at home. She heard the death rattle of the first as she sat at his side. The second, who was only forty-four, woke her in the middle of the night with the chilling rattle she had heard before. A year has passed since Donna lost her second love. "It's been my worst year," she told me, "but I've taken charge of my life. I keep busy, I work, I travel, I enjoy my home, my son and my friends. I date, but another man in my life is not what I look for or want now. Maybe sometime in the future."

Dwelling on harrowing experiences is not healthy and there are ways to overcome them.

Richard, a recent casual acquaintance, lived through one of the most saddening events I can recall. Four years earlier, while driving home from work one evening, he had to stop at an accident scene. He was stunned to learn that the two dead women in the wrecked auto were his daughters. *Horror.*

Richard had lost his wife about a year before the accident. How did he manage his grief and his life? He took on a long-term project. He purchased a huge, dilapidated barn and converted it, detail by detail, into an elegant mansion surrounded by exquisite gardens. One garden, all white, is dedicated to his daughters, another to his wife. Yes, he still mourns, but he's taken charge of his life.

You, too, can take charge of your life!

Regret and Guilt.

> *"If regret is the agony of what you did not do,*
> *guilt is the agony of what you did."*
>
> – Anneli Rufus, contemporary,
> award-winning journalist in
> "The Farewell Chronicles"

These emotions, whether deserved or not, can be self-destructive. You believe you should have done more for the loved one you lost or you have guilt for you may feel that, in some way, you contributed to your loss. Each negative emotion is distressing, but self-induced blame can often be more lasting than others. Guilt, if not checked, may often escalate into self-loathing.

There are ways you can find redemption and achieve *Contentment.*

I experienced both regret and guilt when I was twenty-three and altered forever how I feel and act toward those I love. My mother was most caring and devoted to her three children: my older sister, my younger brother and me. She was manipulative but I loved her dearly. She and my father had a passionate relationship, but they were frequently at odds. They quarreled. My father would often disappear for weeks at a time, not provide for us and left my mother to fend for the family. She was a single parent … rare at the time. It was during the Depression. Times were bad. My mother took odd jobs and kept us afloat. As soon as she graduated from high school, my sister started to work and became the family provider. As time passed, I realized that my mother was controlling my sister and kept her from having a life of her own. After I graduated from college (with my sister's help) and married, they had a falling out. My mother summoned me and pressed me to take on the role of my sister. I clearly remember the incident so many years ago as my mother, standing on the stairway landing in the foyer of her home, looked down on me a few steps below.

I refused, sharply. I was not kind. I would not be manipulated. I was adamant! I had my own life to live.

A year later, my mother was killed in an automobile accident. She was only fifty-four. I was devastated. I felt *guilt* for what I had said … my cruel response to my mother who was in need. I felt *regret* for what I did *not* do. I could have offered to develop a support plan and help reconcile my sister and my mother. Since my mother's death, I make sure I'm there whenever someone I love needs me. I did so for my sister and I have been there for others, as well, several times. Most recently, I placed my own life on hold as I cared for my husband for five years as he was dying of Parkinson's disease.

I'm far from a saint, but I have a sense of redemption and I have overcome the *regret and guilt* by giving a part of myself to those I love.

Susan and Jim, both longtime friends, were preparing for a pool party for neighbors and friends when several guests called at the last minute to accept. Susan checked … hot dogs, hamburgers, ribs, salad, watermelon, wines, soft drinks were plentiful but there were not enough rolls for the barbeque. Always obliging, Jim drove to the bakery and purchased dozens. On his way home his car, was struck head-on by a truck that went out of control when the driver fell asleep at the wheel. Jim was killed instantly.

Susan suffered, she felt she was at fault and experienced *raw* guilt.

She should not have asked Jim to go. She could have done without more rolls. Why hadn't she planned for more in the first place? For months, she continued to blame herself and conjured more reasons how she could have prevented the tragedy. One day, she sensed her two teenage children were slipping away from her. She was brought up short. Finally, she had to admit to herself that they were having their own problems with the loss of their father. They were feeling abandoned by both their parents. Susan told me it was then that she knew she needed help and turned to her pastor. He recommended a widows group where she shared her concerns and finally came to terms with herself. She never completely forgave herself. She focused her attention on her children and slowly, with this necessary dedication, she began to let go of her guilt.

When Ralph and I were building our home in Virginia we became warm friends with **Nora** and Michael, the contractors. They are a devoted couple and have a close family with two adult sons who help operate the business. We enjoyed our home and Nora and Michael visited often. They'd bring McDonald's hamburgers and French fries, we'd supply the drinks and dessert. Lots of fun! When my husband Ralph died, Nora revealed to me that she had been married before and her first husband was the father of her oldest. We never knew. He was a caring man and a rocket scientist with a brilliant future, she said. "When he died we were in our early twenties … I felt *guilt* that it was he, not me. I should have been the one to die. He had so much to offer the world and to live for." Not too long thereafter Michael came into her life. Gradually, Nora overcame her pangs of guilt, remarried and took charge of her life. Her family now includes five grandchildren.

There is another situation that creates guilt in widows. Some hesitate to date, fall in love, enter a relationship or marry because they feel they are betraying the spouse they lost. At times, they experience bittersweet guilt when a gallant comes along and sweeps them off their feet. Often, they do not want to let their lost love go, even after entering a positive union. I have a young man, *much* younger than I, my live-in companion. I have *no* sense of guilt … *but* I do not, I cannot, let Ralph go. Holding on, for me, is comforting and sustaining. It is a choice I have made.

Depression

"Depression or "despair is the rejection of God within oneself."

– Antoine de Saint-Exupéry,
1900-1944, French aviator,
author of "The Little Prince"

Depression can be the most destructive of negative feelings and lead to deeper, more intense mental distress … and sometimes to thoughts of suicide. Most often, depression follows the earlier emotions of shock, grief, sadness, sorrow and anger that you experienced right after your loss. During those early days, weeks or even months the widow, divorcée or betrayed is forced to focus on the pressing needs that require immediate attention ... funeral arrangements, finances and many more. (See section titled The First Days After Your Loss in this chapter on page 19.) Relatives and friends who were there to help and support have drifted away and returned to their own lives. You feel deserted and have to face not only the loss of your loved one, but the void left by those who were at your side through your period of mourning. The sense of being left alone and the anxiety of facing an uncertain future can be overwhelming.

After losing Rudy, her husband of twenty-five years to a debilitating stroke, **Charlene** slipped into deep depression. She suffered several months before deciding to seek help to recover. She called on a psychologist (the only one she knew) she had met at the nursing home where she had visited Rudy every day until he died. The psychologist asked if she would be willing to help some of the other terminal patients in the facility. He said doing so might distract her from her grief. She hesitated. But, desperate, she was determined to try. She learned that many patients never have visitors. She brought members of her church's congregation to visit those with no family. She encouraged neglectful family members to spend time with their ailing relatives. Charlene began to smile herself when she saw smiles on the faces of those she joined together. She went on and called on companies to contribute toiletries and cosmetics in small, colorful packages for patients still able to use them. Charlene not only brings joy to her new friends but has found a sense of joy and peace for herself.

Though depression is becoming more understood and accepted as a

16

treatable mental illness with biological overtones, the general view of this condition as self-inflicted, with a lack of discipline to defeat it, is what most people continue to believe. If you feel you are in a state of depression that is beyond your control, there are professionals who can lead you to recovery. (See CHAPTER 21 on where to look for help.)

What are symptoms of depression?

Depression can be a matter of degree. How strongly do you feel the signs of depression and how long do they last? Are they unrelenting?

*Helplessness, hopelessness, a sense of pointlessness
in the meaning of life.
What is the reason for continuing to go on?
A lack of interest in projects that once occupied
much of your time.
A decline in your health. A loss of desire to eat,
sleep, perform daily tasks.
Continuing thoughts of taking your life.*

A psychiatrist I have known for some time suggests that should you find these symptoms unending and taking over your life, it may be time to seek the counsel of a professional.

Overcoming symptoms:

However, if they are not overwhelming and you are convinced they are temporary but nonetheless sense they are interfering with your taking charge of your life, you may resort to ways to overcome them:

1. If you have gotten this far you have taken the necessary first step in achieving a healthy state of mind. You have accepted your need to set aside your feelings of depression and you have determined you can do it on your own.

2. *Plan.* Set a timetable that will not overtax you and that will give you enough time to complete each step. Prepare a list of what you should do, how much time you should allot to each task and when you will perform it. Such as a half-hour in the morning and/or evening *devoted to yourself.* But don't count on eliminating the symptoms quickly ... give your plan a chance ... a few weeks, maybe more. Just planning will help you take your mind off your

17

problems. Include pleasant indulgences and interject periods of doing work tasks. Start gradually and increase the time to an hour or more as you progress. Pleasant tasks, things you enjoy most: reading, watching a DVD, listening to music, taking a walk, visiting a friend, shopping … anything that gives you a lift. Work tasks: things you've put off, catching up on your e-mail, calling a neglected friend, working on your finances, organizing a bureau drawer, sorting out make-up you no longer use. Exercising can either be an indulgence or a work task but it's one of the best.

3. If you are in a deep negative funk, enjoy an indulgence and make certain the time is spent on you.

4. Record these on your calendar as you would a medical appointment.

Then keep to your schedule!
Don't miss an appointment with yourself!

Most of the chapters in this book
offer tips and suggestions on how to move forward with your plan,
go beyond depression and help you take charge of your life
and achieve Solitary Contentment.

Thoughts of Suicide

Do you have them? Are you looking for a way out of an impossible situation? Do you just want to run away from a deep sense of loneliness or a burgeoning number of insoluble problems? You are not alone. Most are fleeting moments of wishing to escape the ever-present demands of life. The thoughts are common even among those who are well-adjusted and have supportive spouses. However, performing the act never solves the problems.

Often when I feel a need to be comforted, when nothing will help and no one is there for me, I'll talk to the painting of my husband (I talk to him even when I'm not distressed) and ask, "Why did you have to leave me? Why aren't you here to help me through this crisis? *I want to be with you.*" I shed tears. I'm sorry for myself. I go on and on, spilling out what troubles me. Finally, I recover as I recall how fortunate I am to be able to

18

enjoy all the wonderful things life has to offer. It's not always a ride on a cloud, but I survive.

Nicole, one of the divorcées I interviewed, says that when she's at the end of her rope, she takes out a picture of her former husband and, alone, out of earshot of her children and neighbors, she screams at him … she vents her wrath, blames him for her situation … (I'm sure he was at fault) … and she feels much better for it. I'm not one to scream or raise my voice, whether I'm alone or with others. But if it helps you, *go for it.*

In CHAPTER 21 you will also find a list of places and organizations that offer more information as well as where to seek professional counseling.

If you experience any of these or other negative,
harmful and debilitating emotions, acknowledge them,
have a plan to overcome them or seek professional help.
Take charge of your life!

The First Days After Your Loss

The first days after the loss of your loved one are the most distressing, whether sudden or expected. There are two steps you should take immediately that may delay your grieving but will distract you from those first overwhelming days. By *assembling necessary documents* and *making the proper contacts* as soon as possible, you'll also take care of your financial future and well-being.

If you don't know where to turn, contact your county
Probate Court. The name of the court varies from state to state,
i.e., Surrogate Court, Register of Wills and others. The county
administrative office can direct you to the proper court.

Though there were times when my mother and I had our differences, I am ever grateful for what she taught me about living within one's means. It was by her example and cautious comments during the stark days of the Depression that I learned about thrift, saving and meticulous record-keeping.

So, as soon as my husband Ralph and I had saved enough to open a savings account we prepared our first will. A few years later, when we had enough for a down payment, we bought a home with a 4.5 % (low at the time) mortgage and updated the will. Our small family was no different from others of our era … as time passed our lives changed. We had a daughter, acquired a larger property and with the help of a financial adviser we built a modest investment portfolio. It was time to seek the assistance of an attorney to build an estate plan. We were advised to set up trusts to protect our assets and avoid probate. We did all that was required and our plan was updated once again shortly before Ralph died.

We were always current.

Nonetheless, after Ralph's death, it took several months before his estate was settled.

No matter how much planning you do, there are always more forms to be filled out and documents to be acquired and filed. Especially the inescapable tax returns. Even today, I get caught up short when I receive yet another document from my accountant (with an unexpected accompanying bill). Whether you are a widow, divorcée or still married, it is wise to plan ahead as much as possible and be prepared for more later. (You will find how to go about financial planning in CHAPTER 11.)

> *A cautionary note about living trusts: According to*
> *Kevin Hoagland, Middlesex County, New Jersey, Surrogate:*
> *"A last will and testament suffices for most people."*

Step I: Assembling the necessary documents:

Your attorney and/or your contacts will help you determine which documents you will need. It is wise to have the original and at least one copy of each.

1. Estate planning documents:
   The will, trusts and related documents. Even if you have all the necessary documents, you may need an attorney to proceed. If there is no will, you should seek the advice of an attorney and work with the County Surrogate's Office. The state determines

the distribution of assets.

2. Death certificates: you will need several originals.
Copies will not do.

3. Divorce decree

4. Social security numbers and birth certificates of all members of
your family

5. Your marriage license

6. Prenuptial agreement

7. Home/property documents
Deeds
Mortgage documents
Other outstanding debts on your home

8. Auto titles

9. Insurance policies:
Life
Home owners
Auto
Accident
Personal Liability, Umbrella

10. Financial records:
Investments: stocks, bonds, etc.
Bank and brokerage statements
Credit cards
Debt statements
Tax documents: personal, real estate, other

11. Employee insurance and other benefits. Though I was aware that
I had excellent health benefits through Ralph's company, when
I checked with his employer I was surprised to learn that he had
life insurance coverage as well. It was not a large amount, but it
was helpful, particularly at the time. Check your husband's past
employers – there may be payments owed to you.

*Make sure you inquire into all possible sources of benefits, including
the Veterans Administration if he was a veteran*

and professional organizations.

Step II: Your list of sources and contacts:

Though there are some sources and contacts that everyone has, there are others that are unique to you. It is essential that you prepare your list with phone numbers and/or e-mail and/or mailing addresses for quick and easy reference. You may use the documents list as a guide. As soon as possible, you should be in touch with each source to learn exactly which documents are necessary and what is the related deadline.

Be sure to make the contacts and keep the deadlines.
If you don't, you may miss benefits due you.

You may find these two steps tedious and time-consuming
but in the long run they will save you anxiety
and be financially rewarding.

Children Facing the Loss

The loss of a partner by death or divorce is a devastating blow, but it can be even more so for your children. It is a tremendous responsibility on the part of the remaining parent to assure their off-spring that life will continue and be fulfilling, though one of their parents is gone.

For those of us who are baby boomers or older and have lost our husbands, we tend to have grown children who have left the nest and are on their own. An adult child will feel the same emotions of shock and loss. The parent who hugged them, cheered them on, encouraged them, disciplined and counseled them, will no longer be there when they come calling. They will grieve with you. At the same time, grown daughters and sons are generally understanding of the emptiness you now face in your life. They know parents usually die first. They can be comforting and helpful and see you through the trying first days of your grief when you need them most … as well as later. At times, they are more able to cope with the loss since they have their own families, young, with futures, to divert them and to fall back on.

However, if you are a *young* widow or divorcée, you have small children who may not be able to relate yet to the meaning of the true loss or death. Despite your efforts to explain, they may expect their parent to return as he has in the past after a brief business trip or other journey. However, when the reality sets in that he is gone forever, they are overwhelmed with a sense of desertion. They fear that you, too, will abandon them. The weight of your burden is twofold. First, you have your own grief along with the pressure of handling the financial and related details of your loss ... and second, you must reassure your children that you are well and that you love them and will care for them. It is up to you as to how they survive this crisis in your life and theirs. Often, setting up a meeting for all of you with your pastor and/or doctor will be comforting for them.

"Children will respond best if they can understand as much as possible about what has happened to their loved one," writes columnist and psychiatrist Joyce Brothers. "Euphemisms can be confusing or scary, so you should explain the death with as much detail and clarity as the child can understand at his or her age. Talking about death is important, so that the child doesn't learn that it is a taboo subject. It's not wise to talk about the deceased as being asleep. It may confuse the child and make him or her afraid to go to sleep." (Excerpt from a Dr. Brothers column syndicated by King Features Syndicate.)

Among the references available on ways to help
young children understand and cope are sections in
Lynn Caine's "Being A Widow." You will find more details
and references on this and related subjects in CHAPTER 21.

Child-spouse substitutes:

There is often a tendency for a widow or divorcée to rely on a grown child (and even one who is very young) for continuing support and comfort. A divorcée I interviewed told me that she has no need for another husband – her eleven-year-old son is the man of the house. "He's taking it in stride," she insists. Such child-spouse substitutes often cause rifts in the family and have adverse effects on either the mother, the daughter/son or both.

When my father deserted us, my mother became even more caring and protective as a single parent of her three children. She worked diligently. However, she made my eighteen-year-old sister, who was three years older than I, pay for the family's financial needs from the meager salary she was earning. Jean accepted the role as provider, but as years passed and in retrospect, I observed that my mother never relented in her control over my sister and deprived her of a life of her own. After our mother died, Jean led a productive life helping others in the positions she held. She never married. However, she vacillated from occasional *Contentment* to long periods of depression which caused abrupt negative changes in our relationship. Whether she was predisposed to this pattern or whether it was my mother's influence, I am not certain, but I'm sure the latter was a major factor.

The caveat: Filling the shoes of a lost spouse with a child does not necessarily solve short- or long-term problems of a single-parent family … and may create unexpected, complex problems.

There is another side of this coin.

The most refreshing story I have heard about adult children and their love for the remaining parent was recently from a man in his fifties. He had just finished hanging blinds in my foyer and said he was on his way to pick up his mother who was widowed for several years. He had a twinkle in his eyes as he indicated it was his turn to have her stay in his family's home and that he and his two sisters vie for their mother's visits. "After all," he chuckled, "she was my first love!"

Responding to Awkward, Well-Intentioned Remarks

Facing the loss of your loved one is overwhelming enough, but to be expected to respond with grace to clumsy remarks from well-meaning friends can be more than you can bear. You may not be ready to be patient and understanding when your friends make an unintentional, insensitive remark. But it is worth a try to continue the friendship which you may need in the future. Often they've searched for what to say and instead blurt out an offensive comment in an effort to show their concern … and they should be forgiven.

What do you say and how do you respond to, "It's a blessing he's gone, he was suffering so," when you are in agony without him? Or, "What are you going to do with this big house?" Or, "You should go out, soon, and try to find someone else." And others even more personal about how to fill your empty evenings and how to handle your finances and your sex life.

The best way to respond to unsolicited advise, is to be as honest and as direct as you can and calmly, without anger, declare that, "I'm not ready to make that decision" or another similar reply appropriate to the situation. There is no need to apologize or reveal your plans. Being assertive but kind can put you both at ease.

There was a time, a year or more after Ralph died, when I began to enjoy the company of Ken, who is twenty-nine years younger than I. Several friends, mostly women, warned me and expressed concern about his intentions. I smiled and indicated he was sympathetic, understanding and a good friend.

One day, worldly and weathered Bert, who owned a small engine/ large vehicle sales and repair shop, and whom I'd known for some time, came by to drop off my lawn mower. We discussed my property and then switched to my well-being. I mentioned the comments of my friends about Ken, whom he knew. "Victoria," he intoned. "Just remember, that whatever you do in your home is your business not anyone else's."

There are others you know who also have insight and have experienced losses themselves, and ask, "What can we do to help?" They offer to do an errand, invite you to dinner or share an afternoon at a festival or an evening at an outdoor concert or the theater. In time, however, these invitations become fewer or stop, but by then you may have *taken charge of your life* ... or at least have begun to do so.

The rest of the chapters in this book are filled
with ways to achieve Contentment.
In CHAPTER 21 *you will find lists of people, organizations*
and places you can turn to for more information and help.

CHAPTER 3

Are You Prepared for Your New Life? Your Life Alone?

"Life is a series of relapses and recoveries."

– George Ade, 1866-1944,
American writer, columnist, playwright

*T*he funeral is over ... or the final divorce papers have been signed and your ex is gone ... or your betrayer is out of your life! Friends and family have departed. Shock becomes denial. You shudder at the thought of what lies ahead. You are overwhelmed as you try to concentrate on the pressing tasks before you. They mount and grow daunting. Anger, bewilderment, despair, frustration set in.

You have a sense of dismal emptiness.

You are alone.

Your life has just taken a drastic new turn. You wonder, "What should I do now, today, right away ... sell my home, go on an extended vacation, take in a permanent companion, find someone and remarry ... to escape this loneliness?"

Hardly! Don't make another change in your life, yet!

Friends and family often offer to help but do not know what you may need. If anyone suggests a *short* visit at his or her home where you may express your grief, cry and talk about your loss and your sorrow ... or bitterness ... to a sympathetic ear, you may accept and find the comfort you crave and a bridge to your life alone. Nonetheless, it *is wisest*, first, to have assembled the necessary documents as listed in CHAPTER 2 and to have secure knowledge of your financial situation.

(See CHAPTER 11.)

If you choose to go, make sure the invitation is *sincere*. Also try to avoid expecting an early escape haven on your own, because you may be disappointed as I was.

It was two weeks after my husband died ... just after our celebration of his life ... my daughter and her husband, Wayne, had left. I was feeling all those harrowing emotions of loss but most of all I felt deserted and very much alone.

I made a hasty decision that I regretted. I called my daughter and asked if I could spend a few weeks at her home. This, I record in more detail in CHAPTER 5. "I'm very sorry, Mom," she said. (I could sense she was choosing her words carefully.) "My job is making increasing demands on me and I won't be home much of the time. Wayne's situation is the same as mine." Her turndown was a blow that caused me to suffer even greater pain. As time passed ... a long time ... I came to realize that the rejection had served me well. I was put on a path to greater self-reliance, acceptance of my situation, and I was forced to take charge of my life far sooner than I wanted to. More importantly, I learned to avoid making impulsive, imprudent decisions and having unrealistic expectations.

What Does Being Alone Mean to You?

Being lonely? Sad? Isolated? Without friends? Lonesome? Kithless? Kinless? Solitary? Desolate? Abandoned? Forlorn? Azygous? On your own? All of these? None of these? Some of these?

Whatever emotions you experience, you have them because you *are* alone after the loss of your loved one. You will *justifiably* feel one or more of these depressing experiences and that is one of the reasons why I chose to write this book. I hope that among the myriad ways to overcome them which I discuss in the chapters ahead, there are suggestions that will help you find *Solitary Contentment* in the months and years that follow your grieving ... or bitterness. I've been amazed to learn from widows and divorcées I've known or interviewed about how they have grown to accept the condition of being *azygous* with grace and dignity.

Anne, a professor of Women Studies and one of my best friends, suddenly lost her husband of over twenty years to a heart attack. They had been a close, loving couple and together supported many of the university's cultural events. Though I knew she was deeply bereaved, there was an aura of quiet elegance about Anne. She told me her grief counselor suggested she look to her teaching to help her through her crisis. She did ... and reached out further. She added an after-hours class for advanced students ... challenging for Anne and to her benefit and theirs. It was heartening to see my friend confronting and overcoming her aloneness with such grace.

Contemplating the meaning of *azygous*, in itself, can be a distraction from being alone. I had an idea of what it means but to make sure I checked my four-inch-thick Random House Dictionary for a definition. According to Random House, you are *azygous* if you are single, not one of a pair ... so, you are among many who suddenly find themselves *azygous*.

I never experienced the condition of being alone until my husband Ralph died. We had met when we were only seventeen at our college freshman reception, dated for five wonderful years, married and had a happy life together for fifty-eight more. How would I have understood that there is a state of *azygousness*? During the last years of his life Parkinson's disease took Ralph down a cruel, painful path. Toward the end he drifted into dementia and passed on. As I cared for him, loving him more and more each day, I felt an unrelenting hopelessness. He was still with me. But he appeared so very much alone. I did all I could, trying desperately to let him know I was there for him. But neither I nor all the available techniques of modern medical research could save my husband.

Then, he was gone! I was forced to discover what being alone means to me. Ralph was no longer there to talk at supper about how we spent our day, to plan our weekends and vacations, to reminisce about the good times we shared over the years, to kiss hello and goodbye, to feel his body next to me at night, to hold hands as we walked ... and so much more. I learned what aloneness is.

The Emotions and Trials of Being Alone

"In your absence, it is like rising
every day in a sunless sky."

– Benjamin Disraeli, 1804-1881,
Prime Minister to Queen Victoria

Several months passed before I learned that if you find yourself alone, *you need not be lonely or lonesome!* Being alone is a physical situation and it is up to you to decide whether you prolong your grief and languish in self-pity or make a new productive life for yourself. Not only has your loved one left you, but you find you've lost so much more. Of course you will feel the emotions of loneliness, sadness and many others. You are entitled.

There are times when the phone rings and you, as I, expect your loved one is on the other end. Or as you are making breakfast you think he'll walk through the door shortly to join you. Or, it's dinner time and you feel he'll be home soon from work. Or looking out the window and seeing the neighbor's teenage son, instead of your husband, mowing the lawn. Or it's Friday or Saturday night and he'll ask you where you would like to go out for dinner. Each incident causes you to catch yourself up short. He's not there for you anymore.

Then there are the times when you are more than alone, you are lost, near desperation.

It was six months after **McKenzie's** husband Tim died and ten at night in the middle of a winter snowstorm. She was at home alone about to prepare for bed. Suddenly the lights went out. She panicked. She froze. The whirr of the furnace stopped. She feared the temperature would drop. What should she do? She had always counted on Tim for such emergencies. She groped her way to an end table, rummaged in the drawer, found a flashlight and her cell phone.

McKenzie calmed and plunked herself down in a comfortable armchair trying to decide whom to call. Her son? Too far away. A neighbor? Perhaps the outage was in the area? The electric company? An electrician? First, she would find her phone list, and if necessary the phone book. She floundered and the phone slipped out of her hand and fell to the floor. As she scrambled to retrieve it, the lights came back on!

She was relieved. The next time I saw her she told me she learned an important lesson … to be prepared. Her son is briefing her on how to handle the unexpected.

You are fortunate if you were the partner in the relationship who has the inclination, the knowledge and the skills to handle the everyday household utility and appliance failures when they occur. I was not and did not.

My husband Ralph declined slowly so while he was still with me I learned as much as I could about the mysteries of the utilities, the appliances, cars, household systems and outdoor equipment. I never mastered them all so I made my list of experts to call on. What do you do when the washing machine, loaded with laundry, ceases to operate in the middle of its cycle? The mower stops as you try to cut the grass? (All mine needed was some gas.) Then, the clogged toilet, problems with the air conditioner, the refrigerator, the freezer, the furnace, the security system, the phones. If you don't live in an apartment, townhouse or condominium now, you might want to rush and move to one where a quick call to management will solve all your problems (you think). Wait! You're alone … if you make the sudden move to a "carefree community," you may take on new challenges before you're ready and regret leaving behind the comfortable familiar.

More unbearably poignant are the times you are surrounded by family and friends or are in a crowd at a party, a cook-out, a reunion, a church social … but you still feel alone. You've always had your significant other beside you or nearby. True, the hosts and guests all are cordial, bring you into the conversation and try to make you feel included … but *he's* not there. You are uncomfortable as a *single* among couples you used to hang out with, even the ones who've been your neighbors for years or whom you've known since high school or college. The widows and divorcées I know tell me this is the most difficult aloneness they suffer.

You experience these trials and unbearable emotions.
Now is the time to count your blessings (you have them)
and prepare for your life alone!

Preparing for Your Life Alone

You can save yourself costly surprises or the stress of a calamity if you take some time and think through the emergencies your significant other handled. If you're overwhelmed, call on a neighbor, a friend or a member of your family who is handy about the house; he or she will be happy to help the damsel in distress. Ask them (there are women who often fill that role ... my daughter is one of them) for help. Together you can make a list of what to do and whom to contact, with phone numbers, when you have a problem: a plumber, an electrician, the gas company, auto repair shop and more.

If you own your home but do not already have a home warranty contract, purchasing one can be one of the best investments you make. There are companies that provide the service, which covers appliances and home systems repair or replacement for a small fee. This insurance is available on an annual renewal basis and covers: air-conditioners, furnaces, ceiling fans, ductwork, garbage disposals, built-in microwaves, plumbing, ranges, ovens, trash compactors, clothes washers and dryers, well pumps, in-ground pools and spas, dishwashers, electrical systems, garage door openers, cook tops, refrigerator/ freezers and water heaters.

I was fortunate and amazed with the coverage I had which saved me thousands of dollars to correct failing systems in the new home I purchased. But I missed out on one when my garage door opener failed to operate. I didn't think it was covered so I called a repair company and paid for the service. I found out later when I renewed my contract and checked the list ... it is covered. I could have saved even more. Two companies that offer service contracts are American Home Shield AHS and Assurant, Solutions/Service Protection Advantage.

The aloneness, the isolation you feel when you are surrounded by those you have known for years can be overwhelming but can be overcome. You want to be with others who relate to your situation, understand how you feel and have the same sense of loss. Who are they? Where are they? They are *other women*. More and more women are finding themselves alone and in need of companionship. You are a member of this growing segment of the population. Women live longer than men. There are many of us and we are here to help one another.

Stop a moment and remember the women you know who have lost their loved ones ... through death or divorce or betrayal. Call them. They'll know why you did. Invite them to your home. Go out to lunch. Talk. Listen. Go to events together. If you have no women friends nearby, there are places where you'll find them: your church, your college alumnae or alumni association, the Red Hat Society, women's clubs and more. You'll begin to be part of a compassionate group, you'll belong and feel less and less alone.

The Unexpected Gains You Deserve

"I was never less alone than by myself."

– Edward Gibbon, 1734 -1794,
British author, in his Memoirs

Let's leave behind us the *trials and emotions* of being alone, at least for a while!

You've been unhappy! You've been lonely, lonesome and sad.

It's time for you to seek the flip side of being alone ... the pluses! There are several and you deserve to enjoy them. Of course you miss your loved one and would rather have him with you. But he's gone. You do not have to feel guilt when you find something that makes you laugh or someone who makes you happy. **Dr. Serge Kaftal,** of Bernardsville, New Jersey, suggests trying displacement and intellectualization, which internalize your grief and loneliness by substituting positive thoughts and activities. Dr. Kaftal, a family doctor and general practice physician who spends time getting to know and understand each of his patients beyond their obvious complaints, says these techniques can put you on your way to a positive, healthy new way of life.

Displacement: Shifting your grief to a more acceptable,
less threatening emotion, a safer outlet
... redirecting your grief to something else.
Intellectualization: using your intellect (your mind,
your intelligence) to defend against impulses such as grief.

Remember when you watched a televised sports game with your husband and really would rather have turned to *Masterpiece Theatre* on Public Television? You wanted to please him and you did. Now you can always please yourself and turn on any channel that turns *you* on. Or the time you were hoping to try that new French restaurant in the mall and he suggested Italian? Now, if you feel like experiencing the ambience of France, test your French and indulge in escargot, fois gras, a niçoise salad, or the maitre d' special du jour, it's all yours. Or invite a woman friend who also wants to splurge to go with you.

Now, pamper yourself!

Stay up late or go to bed as early as you choose. Get up when you want on the weekend. Schlep around your home in a robe or in the altogether without make-up. Cook your favorite recipes for yourself for any meal, any time. Take a bubble bath and soak until midnight. Stay on the phone forever. Spend more time with women friends and just talk. We women have a knack for talking and listening at the same time.

These are the easy day-to-day pluses that will help you relax, lift your spirits, make you smile or even laugh and *enjoy* being alone. Throughout the rest of this book there are chapters that will help you find ways to experience Dr. Kaftal's displacement and intellectualization techniques which bring you long-term satisfaction. They take time, planning and effort, but you will find *Contentment* you may never have believed possible.

Making the Decision to Remain Alone

"He may well win the race who runs alone."

– Benjamin Franklin, 1706-1790,
diplomat, printer, scientist,
in "Poor Richard's Almanac"

The choice to live your life alone without a partner is not an easy one to make and should only be made after you spend months or years of exploring and contemplation.

After **Daisy,** a successful real estate agent, was widowed in her early fifties, she had several gallants who wooed her and some who asked her to marry. She settled on one, not to marry or live with, but as a companion. She and her guy, Joe, enjoyed a happy monogamous relationship ... separately. He'd stay a few days with her in the Cape Cod cottage she had shared with her husband. Occasionally, she visited Joe in his twelve-room mansion with pool. Though she and Joe had many good times together, as years went by Daisy began to feel suffocated. She wanted to be free to pursue her own interests, alone. After twelve years and to Joe's surprise, she called off their "affair," has settled in a smaller, cabana-like dwelling near her daughter and has found *Contentment.*

Within a year after her husband's passing, **Laurie,** in her forties, alone and vulnerable, was conned by a handsome, smooth talker into a live-in situation in a distant farm community. She sold her house in the city and made the move. Just two months later, he asked her and her teenage daughter to move out. After she left, she learned he had treated two other women the same way. The experience made Laurie cautious. She attended a community singles club and met John, who was a reliable, hardworking professional. They married and have spent several good years together in his trim ranch house on a three-acre lot. John has since retired, is declining in health and leaves the care of the property to Laurie, who is a healthy seventy-something. Laurie endures but would like to move into a carefree townhouse, *alone.*

Among the saddest cases I have encountered is **Terry,** another woman who *wants* to be alone. She's neither widowed nor divorced. She's been in an unhappy marriage for three decades and does volunteer work when she can get away from her neglectful, domineering husband. She wants to live alone but doesn't know how to escape from her imprisonment. And, she refuses to seek counseling.

Judy, widowed for twenty-five years, lives alone and has an active social and volunteer life. There has never been another special man in her life since her husband died. However, she says with a twinkle in her eyes, if the right one were to come along, one who is at least ten to fifteen years younger than she, and is relatively attractive with a decent head of hair, she wouldn't hesitate to leave her life alone to join him. Since there's no one on the horizon to fill her ideal she contentedly continues a very busy life on her own.

When I moved into my new home (alone), **Heather,** the social director of the fifty-two unit townhouse community, called on me with a welcome gift. She was, and is, bubbly, cheerful and chatty. As I learned to know her, I found her joy boundless and contagious. I also learned that she had lost two husbands, one to divorce; the second with whom she had a loving marriage had died five years earlier. As volunteer social director, she coordinates two annual parties ... if no one else offers to hold the Christmas event, she has it at her home ... this year it rained the day of the pool party, so it was at Heather's. She holds smaller gatherings in between. Heather is an avid photographer, taking photos of everything and everyone. The walls of her home ... and the door of her refrigerator ... are covered with the colorful prints. There's more ... she travels six months of the year, visiting her children and grandchildren and touring exotic places. Her latest was Dubai. She has found more than *Contentment*. She has achieved *Excitement!* Heather just turned seventy. *Beat it!*

> *"As you face your life alone, contemplate this mantra:*
> *Inside myself is a place where I live all alone and*
> *that's where I renew my springs that never dry up."*
>
> – Pearl S. Buck, 1892-1973,
> Nobel Prize winning author

CHAPTER 4

Have an Identity Crisis?
Learn How to Get to
Know Yourself!

*"No one can make you feel inferior
without your consent."*

– Eleanor Roosevelt, 1884-1962.
First Lady and UN delegate

One of America's most celebrated writers, **Maya Angelou,** knows who she is and *has taken charge of her life.* Her crowning moment as a poet, she declares, is when she delivered a poem she wrote for President Bill Clinton at his inaugural on January 20, 1993. Born in 1928, Angelou had to deal with several traumas throughout her life … her parents' divorce, her rape and her identity as a black woman. Not only did she endure, but she prevailed and is in complete control of her destiny.

Seeking Your Own Identity

You, too, can be a *phenomenal* woman

As women, we are, by nature, trusting and nurturing human beings. Of course there are exceptions. Most of us, however, are the warm, caring ones. We bond with our significant others and become as one with a singular identity or (not a recommended choice) we surrender our "self" completely. Suddenly, because our partner has died, left or betrayed us we find ourselves without that covenant. Bewildered, we wonder, "Who am I?" "What do I want?" "What do I need?" "How can I go it alone?"

37

A realization strikes us: If we want to take charge of our lives
we must have our own identities.

Strangely, the loss of a loved one and being left alone is an opportunity to uncover the "self" you never thought you wanted or knew existed. You *can* achieve the self-image you deserve. Start with the qualities you already have, slowly build on your growing self-confidence and learn who you really are and decide who you want to be.

You may start by using the list below.

Try to perform all of the fifteen categories. However, you may find your identity after finishing just a few. Start with the first and go down the list or select the categories that will best fill your special needs.

This procedure will help you take stock of yourself and make the most of your redeeming qualities. Make your own lists, as suggested. As you progress, you may, strangely, find several of which you have been completely unaware come to light. If you *discover* some negatives, adjust, correct or cross them off and concentrate on the *positives*. As you go through this list and learn of problem situations or projects that interest you, *check the chapters that follow for information to help find your identity.*

1. *Your Health:* This is a good place to start. Check with your doctor to learn how well you are and if you have a condition that should be treated so you can proceed with the assurance that you are well.

2. *Your Family:* Are the members of your family supportive? If so, this is a big plus. List the ones you can rely on and what they do for you.

3. *Your Finances:* Are you in control of your finances? Or, are you working toward that end? Or will a professional be helpful? (See CHAPTER 11.)

4. *Your Friends:* Evaluate your friendships and list those you can count on and what they have to offer you (and you to them). Being there for someone else can be more   rewarding than seeking help for yourself. Just one good friend can fill your needs.

5. *Your Home:* Look around your home and discover the places where you find solitude and a sense of well-being. Or would you rather be someplace else? If so, plan a move, but delay any decision until you have established your self-image.

6. *Your Appearance:* Gaze upon your face and your figure in a full-length mirror. Make a list of your best features. Be honest! Believe it or not, you have several. Make the most of them. Everyone tells me I have great legs, so I wear short skirts. Play up the great, and down the not so great. Plan to improve the latter. A new hairdo, exercise to tone flabby muscles, some new clothes to get a racier look.

As you consider the next three categories make sure you take time to think them through. Are they your own choices, or have you acquired them over the years you spent with your spouse and compromised to please him? I watched "Sing Along With Mitch" with my husband Ralph though I preferred "Masterpiece Theatre," which he would watch with me. I like a white pasta sauce, but I made marinara sauce because it was his choice. I'd attend social events with his staid scientist friends and even have fun, but I prefer writers, editors, theater people and artists. We wanted to please each other and were happy to concede. However, after Ralph died, I sought my own identity. I focused on my own likes and dislikes and along with other considerations, I found my identity. Now, you are seeking yours ... make certain your likes, dislikes and can't-stands are definitively your own and not acquired. Doing so will be a giant step toward establishing your own identity.

7. *Your Likes:* Music. TV programs. Films. Food. Dining out. Reading. Gardening. (My husband and I split the chores at our home, he did the outside work. I took care of the house. When he became ill I did the gardening too. I learned that not only do I like to work with plants and flowers, they have become a passion for me.) Types of men and women: talkative, witty, introverted, good listeners. Exercise. Walking. Hiking. Pets. And many more. Make your list and pursue the ones you like best.

8. *Your Dislikes:* Use the same items as in *Your Likes.* Make your list and avoid them.

9. *Your Can't-Stands:* Sloppily dressed men. Telemarketing calls. Getting up early every morning. Barley soup. (I hate it.) Standing in line at the post office – anywhere. Gossiping (or is it a like?) Living in the country, the city. Make your list and avoid them like the fury.

10. *What Makes You Happy?* Spending time with your children/ grandchildren. Holidays with your family. Taking a walk with your puppy. Meditating. List them, include them all. Do them.

11. *What Makes You Sad?* The absence, of course, of your loved one. Not hearing from a good friend. Learning that a friend is ill or has died. The loss of a pet. List others. Being sad is okay, but don't let it consume your life.

12. *Your Personality:* Be honest in all your answers, particularly for this one. Don't be hard on yourself with this category. You do have great qualities. List them. Whether you're shy or outgoing, tongue-tied or talkative, low-key or enthusiastic, sociable or aloof, in control or hot-tempered, fun-loving or sullen … other. None are either good or bad. They are a matter of degree and contribute to the whole person of who and what you are. Acknowledge them. They are part of your identity.

13. *Your Job:* If you have one that's great. If you enjoy it that's even better. If you don't like it, list the good and the bad about your job and decide if you should change. If you don't have a job, consider finding one.

14. *Your Sex Life:* More than likely it doesn't exist right now because you've lost your loved one. But if you have ever felt sexy, you're sure to find a partner. If you are no longer interested, or think it's too soon, just wait a while. You'll be surprised how those desires will all come back.

15. *Are You Assertive?* If you don't believe you are, believe you can be. It will help your self-image to be assertive … not aggressive. *Just try.* Be assertive whether you are convinced you can or cannot be. Play-act. By trying again and again you'll find that, by sheer repetition, you've taken hold and that, indeed, you have become assertive.

I don't necessarily concur with former President Bill Clinton's comment on this subject, but what he believes is worth a moment of thought. A tough guy usually prevails, Clinton has declared in debates, because it's "better to be wrong and strong than weak and right."

When you make your lists, keep the good answers and eliminate the not so good. Concentrate on the positive ones. You will realize that you have more to start building toward your self-image than you believed when you started. Rely on a worthy mantra:

Count your blessings and move forward.

Remember to check the Table of Contents for chapters
with information that will expand your search for your identity
and help you achieve Contentment
alone or with another significant other.

CHAPTER 5

A Cautionary Tale:
Go Slowly, Set Goals, Have a Plan

"Patience is passion tamed."

– Lyman Abbott, 1835-1922,
American clergyman, editor

$\mathcal{D}$*on't do it, yet!*

Don't sell your home, take a new job, accept a sudden marriage proposal, discard treasures with painful reminders of happier times or make any major, and in some cases even a minor change you feel driven to undertake! Not yet!

*Changes are filled with challenges and unknowns
and are best approached slowly and with caution.*

Shirley put her condominium on the market right after her husband's funeral and moved in with her son and his family … they wanted her and she is fond of them. Even with a mother-in law suite of her own, she soon realized she wasn't prepared to be a live-in babysitter in a noisy, lively household. She was fortunate that her own home had not yet been sold when she decided to move back to quiet, familiar surroundings.

However, you can *start* to pursue your project by taking steps slowly to assure your transition is smooth and your move is successful. And that the change you've chosen is the right one for you. Your decisions should be made from strength, not from the panic of loss and loneliness.

The place to begin, if you've not already done so, is by establishing your identity and self-confidence as discussed in CHAPTER 4: *Have an Identity Crisis?* With your identity in place, you are ready to make plans for taking the next steps toward your new life and launching the changes you crave.

There are chapters in this book that can help you identify the Contentment opportunities you may wish to undertake and how you may go about achieving them.
Now, begin!

"Be patient as a gentle stream."
– William Shakespeare

First: Prepare *a list of changes you want to make or projects you want to undertake.* Select two or three, then eliminate all but one. Take time to make sure you are making the right choice. What are your passions? You have them and this is your opportunity to carry them out. Do not take on more than one at a time. After you accomplish one, you can always go on to another. Or you might want to proceed with a short-term project and then take on one that's long-term. Review your decisions carefully … a smaller home, a new job, a short- or long-term vacation, moving in with a friend, seeking a lover … be sure that the path you've chosen is, indeed, the best one for you.

Be ready for disappointments and be prepared to substitute another choice.

I learned … after I rushed in and acted on my first decision right after the celebration of my husband's life.

I should have taken time, care and thought before I proceeded. I was hurt, badly. But I recovered. This story is long in its telling but it taught me … go slowly, weigh your options carefully … and, it was up to me, *I had to take charge of my life* … as you must take charge of yours.

When my husband Ralph and I first were told that he had Parkinson's disease I did not realize its seriousness. The doctors did not go into detail. Though I pored over books and articles on the subject, I was still unaware. We continued our plans to move from New Jersey to the country in Virginia and build our Georgian home on the side of a mountain. Lisa, our daughter, and her husband, Wayne, expressed concern because a five-hour drive would separate us. I told them we'd be fine. We were. I managed even as Ralph declined. Together we enjoyed our new home and the area's arts community. Two years later, stressful incidents began to occur. When Ralph faltered, Lisa rushed down to be at my side. The last time it happened, shortly before he died, she helped me find a nursing home where he would be comfortable and cared for with compassion.

Within a month and a-half he was gone.

Lisa and Wayne spent several days with me. They were supportive and helpful. We reviewed estate planning documents and organized the memorial celebration in our home, which was a moving tribute to my husband. Then, they left.

I was not ready to cope with all "the first days after loss" projects. I felt a deep gray emptiness. Why not visit my daughter for a week or two ... she understood how close Ralph and I had been and how much I missed him.

It was then that I made my hasty decision.

I called Lisa. There was a long silence after I told her my plan. I could tell she was choosing her words carefully. "I don't think that's a good idea, Mom," she began. "Oh?" I breathed heavily to myself. "Wayne and I won't be home very much ... we have our jobs, we often work late and would not have time to spend with you." I didn't tell her that I wouldn't mind. Just being there in friendly surroundings, away from painful reminders, would be comforting. And we could spend some time together in the evenings. I did not express what I felt. I hesitated. "Perhaps you're right," I said as bravely as I could muster. We talked a few minutes longer and said warm so-longs.

I was hurt. I felt rejected, alone.

I suffered. I grieved for Ralph and felt abandoned by my daughter. I spent lonely, sleepless nights trying to understand why ... for Lisa was always there for me. Finally, after several bitter days, I knew I had to overcome those debilitating emotions. I forced myself to focus on the "first days" projects. I attended church for the first time in years. I considered long-term goals and a short-term distraction. I needed to get away, any place, some place. Why not a trip? I always enjoyed travel and exploring new places. I started to plan. This time I was not hasty.

I took time to weigh the options, where to go, when, and which would be most distracting and would give me the most peace of mind and *Contentment*. I decided on a Mediterranean cruise. I found the perfect deal on the Internet and in three months I was on my way. Alone.

My choice was gratifying and fulfilling. The weather was perfect, the ship was small and luxurious, the service impeccable. The passengers were friendly but not intrusive. I enjoyed several of the land tours. On the deck, particularly in the evenings, I looked out over the sea and contemplated my long-term projects. In retrospect, my daughter, I concluded, was right. She had her own life to live and I had to make my own. Though, of course, I felt rejected at the time, it was she who made me realize that it is I, not she, who must take charge of my life. The sooner I started, the sooner I would find *Contentment*.

You don't need to take a cruise, though there are many affordable ones to choose from. Consider a week at the shore, or a bed and breakfast at a lake. Or explore an historic site. Williamsburg, Virginia is a great getaway. If you don't know where to go, call your state's tourism bureau for places nearby. You'll find the short time you are away will be uplifting and refreshing and put you on the path to your new life. You will be more prepared to make long-term choices.

By being patient and moving cautiously
you can avoid the mistakes Shirley and I made.

Second: You know what change you will make, now analyze the *reasons why* you made this choice. A new home … your current one is too large, your finances can't maintain it. A new job …. to increase your income or your current one is no longer challenging. A vacation … you need to get away, or want to find new friends. I went on the cruise to seek my identity and start to plan my future.

Lillian analyzed her lifestyle after her husband died. Her nest was empty, without the love of her life, it was very empty. Her property was professionally landscaped with a pool, which her husband had maintained. Without his income and not being an outdoors person she chose to move into a townhouse. She proceeded slowly, made lists of pros and cons and discussed her move with an attorney and a real estate broker. They confirmed that her choice was sound.

46

Once you have made your choice(s)
and have good reasons to support it (them),
take a deep breath and move on to the next step.

Third: Since you have determined which change or project you will undertake, it's time to move on and develop *an inventory* of what you have to offer or need to ensure your move will be a success. Dig into the resources you may not even know you have. Make a list of your interests, your likes and dislikes, motivations, creative talents and other qualities you have that will support your choice.

Katharine Meyer Graham had spent twenty-three years as a homemaker and mother of four children when her husband, Philip Graham, publisher of *The Washington Post*, committed suicide. She drew upon skills and strengths she had never used before (and perhaps was unaware that she possessed) to operate the business and to secure the future of the newspaper for her family. Despite the skepticism of those in the financial community, she became one of the foremost leaders (not just among women) in publishing during the twentieth century.

You may have chosen to start a business of your own ... in decorating. You've decorated your home more than once, you know the market. You've handled the family finances. You have friends who have asked you for advice. How about a catering business or tutoring service? Have a little nest egg? Go for it!

Whatever your choice, make sure it is supported by definitive resources. The most often sought changes are finding a new job and moving to a new home. You will find detailed information on these subjects in CHAPTERS 16 and 19.

Fourth: Now you are ready to develop your plan ... akin to a business plan. Be sure you consider the following:

- Your purpose

- Your goals: What do you hope to accomplish?

- Where will you carry it out: home, new city, college, library ... ?

- How will you carry it out: phone, personal contact, e-mail, Internet ...?

- What other resources do you need besides your own?

- Will taking a course be helpful? If yes, what kind?

- Are your finances sufficient or do you need a loan?

- How much time do you need to allocate to each part of your plan?

- Do you have a friend, or friends to call on for help?

- What type of professional assistance do you need: attorney, accountant, agent, organization?

- Are there items to review that are unique to your project?

Fifth: This last step, *setting a realistic timetable* for your change, can be the most critical to achieving your goal(s). Have patience. Don't be hasty. You will experience disappointments when you do not meet expectations that you set to achieve too early. You may destroy your confidence and void your entire project. Be guided by Shakespeare's caveat, *"Be patient as a gentle stream."*

> *"Whatever you can do or dream you can, begin it.*
> *Boldness has genius, power and magic in it.*
> *Begin it, now."*

> – Johann Wolfgang von Goethe,
> 1749-1832, philosopher

Good luck.

Remember to check the chapters in this book that can help you identify the Contentment options you may wish to undertake and how you may go about achieving them.

CHAPTER 6

Your Health and Exercise

"Health is the Vital Principle of Bliss
and Exercise, of Health!"

> – James Thomson, 1700-1748,
> Scottish poet from
> "The Castle of Indolence"

*W*ant to get on the path to good health? *Interact with friends,*
women friends!

Though my daughter Lisa knew that I was writing this book, she
was unaware of which subject I was working on from day to day. By
strange coincidence, as I started to research *Your Health and Exercise,* she
sent me the following e-mail ... an appropriate opening for this chapter:

> *An evening class at Stanford University focuses on the mind-*
> *body connection – the relationship between stress and disease.*
> *The speaker (head of psychiatry at Stanford) said, among other*
> *things, that one of the best things a man could do for his health is*
> *to be married to a woman, whereas for a woman, one of the best*
> *things she could do for her health was to nurture her relationships*
> *with her girlfriends.*
> *At first everyone laughed, but he was serious.*
> *Women connect with each other differently and provide*
> *support systems that help each other to deal with stress and*
> *difficult life experiences. Physically, this quality "girlfriend time"*
> *helps us create more serotonin – a neurotransmitter that helps*
> *combat depression and can create a general feeling of well-being.*
> *Women share feelings whereas men often form relationships*
> *around activities. They rarely sit down with a buddy and talk*

about how they feel about certain things or how their personal lives are going. Jobs? Yes. Sports? Yes. Fishing, hunting, golf? Yes. But their feelings? Rarely.

Women do it all the time. We share from our souls with our sisters/mothers, and evidently that is very good for our health. He said that spending time with a friend is just as important to our general health as jogging or working out in a gym.

There is a tendency to think that when we are "exercising" we are doing something good for our bodies, but when we are hanging out with friends, we are wasting our time and should be more productively engaged – not true. In fact, he said that failure to create and maintain quality personal relationships with other humans is as dangerous to our physical health as smoking!

So every time you hang out to schmooze with a gal pal, just pat yourself on the back and congratulate yourself for doing something good for your health! We are indeed very, very lucky. Sooooo, let's toast to our friendships. Evidently, it's very good for our health.

Therefore, if you schmooze regularly with your girlfriends you *are* on your way to a healthy lifestyle.

Are you ready to start or resume a good health plan?

You have had little or no time to focus on your wellbeing because you still may be grieving. Nonetheless, you may be eager to move on.

You have just discovered what friendships with women can do for you. Here in this chapter, you will find more factors that will help you achieve your goal of good health. Next on the list is a physical exam. Then, no one denies that exercise and diet are "vital principles" to one's health. There are more: sleep, attitude, an active mind and laughter. These elements overlap, with each as important as the other. Promise yourself to take the time to make them all a part of your "good health regimen."

Your physical examination

You are fortunate if you already have a doctor who will give you the personal attention and the *complete* physical exam you should have. If you don't, contact a local medical center or the community hospital in your area for recommendations. Make sure the doctor understands your situation. Discuss your planned regimen with him or her. Don't hesitate to get a second opinion if you are uncertain about your interview or the exam. When you leave or soon after your exam, you should know the state of your health and what type of treatment plan you need, if any.

In addition to regular physical examinations and a wide variety of advanced specialty care, the **Mayo Clinic**, which has facilities in Arizona, Florida and Minnesota, also offers an Executive Health Program. The plan is comprehensive, lasts two or three days and includes complete blood count and chemistry, urinalysis, coronary risk/lipid panel, chest x-ray, mammography, pelvic exam, cardiovascular (heart) evaluation, colon cancer screening, audiogram and more. The consultations and screenings are tailored to your specific needs. These Mayo Clinic programs are worth considering.

There are other tests that are *not routine* but can prevent or predict tendencies to conditions such as heart attacks, strokes, cancer, diabetes, Alzheimer's, ulcers and eye disorders. They include an aspirin check, tests for CRP or C-reactive protein, vitamin D level, a test for an H. pylori infection or your insulin level.

These are some of the available tests that you can discuss
with your physician to determine which to include in your exam.

Exercise

Of all the factors in a health plan, exercise is the most time-exacting, but ultimately is worth the investment. You may wish to start because you have an objective: lose weight, tone your body, trim your tummy, get back in shape, or just feel good about yourself. You know you should. You should, because you deserve it. Also, there are health benefits with proper programs that will lower the risk of heart disease, high cholesterol, cancer, depression and other diseases.

Regardless of which system you choose,
be sure to check with your doctor first to determine
if you are ready, physically, mentally and emotionally.

Unless you are determined to have a rigorous regimen right away, start with something simple and move on later to a more inclusive

51

program. An easy way to prepare for those strenuous workouts is what you do all the time … but do more of it … *walking* … walking at a fast pace and on a regular schedule. Start with thirty minutes, three times a week: early morning, noon or evening. Increase it to forty-five minutes everyday with a few stretches at the end. You may choose to continue this routine and/or elect to take on more.

There are dozens of options out there and it is worth taking time to research the best way for you to proceed. You can find exercise programs that you can undertake at home on the Internet, in magazines and books. You may check your local community fitness centers, register for one of their courses and make use of their equipment. It is up to you as to when, where and what direction you want to take. You may select what fills your objective and do it on your own … or call on a trainer who will analyze your physical condition and recommend the fitness program that he or she may tailor for you.

Among the available established programs are two that are popular and each has millions of enthusiasts: *Pilates* and *Zumba*. Interestingly, both were inspired, in part, by dance and have also influenced leaders in that field, among them George Balanchine, to integrate some of the exercises in their routines.

Pilates is named after its German physical-culturist founder, ***Joseph Pilates.*** He began as a circus performer and went on to become a boxer and an instructor of self-defense. He studied Eastern and Western philosophies and was influenced by Greek and Roman exercise regimens. Pilates was born in 1880 and developed his routines as a young man to heal his body of ailments he suffered, which included asthma, rickets and rheumatic fever. After World War II he moved to New York City, where he opened his first studio. Here, he continued his passion for body-building, gymnastics and other physical precepts. Not only did he create over six hundred exercises, he invented apparatus that are designed to condition the entire body. ***Mary Alldian,*** Pilates instructor at the Hunterdon Health and Wellness Center in Clinton, New Jersey, says the core of his philosophy "is based on mat work, which focuses on achieving good health by addressing the whole being … breath, body, mind and spirit. Pilates systems offer numerous benefits that influence many aspects of physical fitness: strength, flexibility, coordination, speed, agility, endurance and balance in one's life."

If you choose to pursue the Pilates method or just want to read about a system that has been proven over several decades and is practiced and taught worldwide, obtain a copy of the book, *Pilates,* by Rael Isacowitz. The four-hundred-thirty-three-page volume contains two-hundred-and-five exercises, conveniently organized and superbly illustrated. You may develop a Pilates program on your own, but better yet, try to work with an experienced personal Pilates trainer.

Zumba also practiced and taught all over the world, is a fitness program with dance, musical overtones and a contemporary beat. According to the system's originators, it is "an exhilarating, effective, easy-to-follow, Latin-inspired, calorie-burning dance fitness party." It was developed by happenstance in the mid 90s by Colombian choreographer and dancer, **Alberto "Beto" Perez.** In a rush to be on time to teach an aerobics class in his native Cali, Colombia, Perez left behind his traditional aerobic music. With tapes of salsa and merengue music he had in his backpack, he improvised. The room was electrified with a burst of energy. The students loved it.

The *Zumba Fitness Party* was born and quickly spread throughout Colombia. In 2001, with two entrepreneurs, both also Colombians and named Alberto, Perez set up studios in Miami, Florida. The company grew worldwide and expanded to include apparel, accessories, CDs and a best-selling home fitness DVD series, the *Zumba Fitness Total Body Transformation System.* If a dance fitness program excites you, you may join a class in your area taught by licensed Zumba instructors or do-it-yourself at home with a Zumba DVD.

Once you have launched your exercise regimen,
not only will you be on your path to good health,
you will build your energy and self-esteem!

A Healthy Diet

There are scores of diet plans available to help you lose weight. This chapter-section is *not* designed to help you lose or gain weight. It suggests how you may attain and maintain good health. A healthy diet requires healthful food to support good health. Simply, if you want good health, eat healthful foods. Here are a few general healthful food tips:

- Cut back or eliminate fatty food.

- Drink lots of tea. There are hundreds of varieties. Choose greens and caffeine-free. But all have benefits. Most have cleansing, stimulating effects, are high in antioxidants and help reduce LDL (bad) cholesterol.

- Limit (or omit if you can) the amount of red meat you eat.

- Indulge in fruits and vegetables. Leafy greens like lettuce, endive, spinach and romaine and colors, the stronger the better … blueberries, raspberries, tomatoes.

- Instead of butter, use olive oil and canola oil.

- Include legumes in your meals. Beans, peas and lentils help lower LDL cholesterol.

- Fill up on fish. The Omega-3 fats in seafood help prevent heart disease.

- Nibble nuts in moderate amounts. They provide healthy fats; try walnuts, almonds, pistachios.

- Have a glass of purple grape juice or red wine every day.

- Substitute herbs or spices for flavor in place of salt, sugar and fat.

- Switch to low-fat or no-fat milk and yogurt.

- Eat often, three light meals and two snacks a day.

Following these tips will provide you with the benefits of fiber, minerals, antioxidants, vitamins and help keep your immune system healthy. They will help lower your cholesterol and help protect you against a full range of cancers, including lung and breast cancer, heart disease, osteoporosis and diabetes.

If you feel you want help for a special problem or disorder, seek out a nutritionist who will design a diet or program to respond to your need.

A Good Night's Sleep

Coping with the stress and pressures caused by the loss of your loved one can keep you from getting a good night's rest when you need it most. According to **Dr. Mary Susan Esther,** former president of the American Academy of Sleep Medicine, "Getting good sleep boosts your energy, your mood and your concentration." Having a sleep-wakeup routine can help you fall asleep and stay asleep throughout the night. Try going to bed and rising at the same time every day. After a while your body establishes a rhythm and should fall naturally into your pattern. You may also sprinkle sleep-inducing scents on your freshly washed bed linens … like lavender water, vanilla and green apple. Have a good snooze every night.

Attitude

"If you think it, it will."

The concept that thought and prayer can heal has been with us since the beginning of time. Today it is supported by scientific research and data. Studies have proven there is a link between stress and disease. The field of psychoneuroimmunology (how neurological and immune systems interact) shows evidence of a relationship between thoughts and health. In other words, your thoughts can control your physical being. Imagery can make us ill. It can also help us heal. So think positive thoughts.

When you feel your grief is overwhelming or you face an all-consuming task, take time out. Cuddle up in a comfortable upholstered chair, lie down on a soft couch or in your bed. Close your eyes. Imagine the happiest, most relaxing time you have experienced in your life. Lying in the sun on the beach. On a chaise on the deck of a ship, looking out over a calm, azure sea. The best holiday you had with your family. There is scientific proof that your happy thoughts will influence your body and mind to respond positively and you will heal. Try it, you'll like it!

Laughter

Laugh a lot. Laughter is contagious. A hearty laugh is good for your health, your mind, your soul and your body. Laughter sets off the release of endorphins, natural good feeling chemicals that give you a sense of well-being. Laughter is the cheapest medication. It's free. When you laugh, you pump more oxygen into your lungs and improve your blood flow. Thus you boost your immunity, relax your muscles, decrease pain and relieve your stress. Best of all, you bring zest and joy to your life.

55

An Active Mind

Be alert. Read. Write. Keep a journal of what you do and record your feelings and emotions. Read a newspaper rather than relying on television for the news. Keep current with what is going on in your community, your state and the world. Take an adult course in a subject you've always wanted to learn fully. Use your computer. Try to keep up with as much of the trends in technology as you can. You needn't be a computer geek, but you should try to absorb what you can about the latest developments. Nor do you have to carry out all of these suggestions ... but do enough to keep your mind active and healthy.

Conclusion

Your health is your top priority. All the factors in this chapter will help you maintain a healthy life-style . Some take more time than others. Start with the easiest and take on one at a time. Practice it a week or two. Then add another until you are comfortable with carrying out all (or most) of them on a regular basis. For more factors that lead to good health, see CHAPTER 7: *Handling Stress* Reread it or read it for the first time. Eliminating stress contributes to your health and well-being.

Go for it!

CHAPTER 7

Handling Stress:
Create "My Place" for Meditation
and Relaxation

*"Stress is invisible but omnipotent. It steals
the bloom from the cheek, it takes away
the appetite and turns the hair gray."*

Benjamin Disraeli, 1804-1881,
Queen Victoria's Prime Minister

Stressed Out?

Want to make your stress melt away? You can refresh your body and spirit and find the *Contentment* and joy you had before you lost your loved one. *Or have you ever experienced such happiness?* Performing just some of the steps you'll find in this chapter will help you relax, laugh, appreciate the wonders of living, be happy to be alive and find peace and serenity. Practice them for a few minutes a day and enjoy these uplifting sensations. Do some or all of them often and they will encompass your entire life and lighten the stress for short or long periods of time and perhaps for always.

The world around you won't change. You will still be alone. But your mind will be clear and more alert, you will be relaxed and your energy restored. You will be better prepared to meet the challenges of your loss.

*Let's first explore the symptoms of stress
and the dangers of
letting them get out of control!*

Do You Have the Symptoms and Manifestations of Stress?

There are few of us who don't.

The dictionary definition of *stress* is "the state of extreme difficulty, pressure and strain." The elements of stress manifest themselves in many ways.

Physical effects: feelings of tenseness and nervousness, stomach pains and related disorders, diarrhea and constipation, headaches, heart palpitations and sleeping problems.

Emotional effects: crying often; sudden outbursts of anger; a loss of interest in sex; indulging in drinking, eating, spending or gambling; an uncontrollable irritability with events you used to be able to handle or overlook and a desire to escape responsibilities.

Mental effects: confusion, an inability to concentrate, momentary loss of memory, difficulty in expressing yourself.

You don't experience all of these symptoms and not all the time. But even one or two for a short period can take a toll on your health. Many are common, particularly when you try to cope with the demands of facing life without your spouse or betrayer … the funeral, the divorce, the details of preparing estate documents, adjusting to being alone, consoling your children, juggling demands of daily life you used to share, handling finances and many more.

What happens when you let stress take control of your life?

> *"Despair (stress) is a mental state which exaggerates*
> *not only our misery but also our weaknesses."*

Luc de Clapiers,
Marquis de Vauvenarques, 1715-1748
in "Reflexions"

If you permit stress to take over your life, you may develop physical conditions that require medical attention. According to **Nancy Ferrari,** managing editor of the Harvard Medical Publications, untreated symptoms of stress can lead to chronic physical illnesses such as heart disease, high blood pressure, lingering respiratory disorders and gastro-intestinal conditions. These physical illnesses are more difficult to treat than the stress itself. They can grow worse and shorten one's life. Therefore, when you find your symptoms of stress are getting out of hand it's wise to seek professional advice to prevent potential debilitating physical disorders.

In his best selling book, *The Relaxation Response,* **Dr. Herbert Benson,** *founder of the Harvard Mind/Body Institute* and Associate Professor of Medicine at the Harvard Medical School, attributes lower blood pressure, slower breathing and reduced heart rates to proper stress management techniques.

Now, to the ways on ...

How You Can Make Stress Melt Away

> *"The beauty of the world has two edges, one of laughter,*
> *one of anguish (stress)cutting the heart asunder."*

Virginia Woolf, 1882-1941, author, in
"A Room of One's Own," 1929

There are three basic procedures, as detailed in this chapter, for reducing and managing stress: *conscious breathing, relaxation postures* and *meditation.* The place where you practice these components can be as important as the exercises themselves, particularly for meditating. As you begin your healing process, you will feel more at ease if you meditate in a place you create ... a room, a corner, a nook ... that is quiet, comfortable and remote, away from your everyday pressures. Later, as you conquer the routines, you will be able to repeat some of them even in the presence of others, without their knowledge: as you take a walk, sit at your desk, ride in a bus, train or a plane, during a concert or a theatrical performance, waiting for a medical appointment. Wherever you practice them, they will help you keep in touch with your emotions and achieve the relaxation, healing, restoration and *Solitary Contentment* you crave. (*A double caveat:* Do not undertake any of these techniques while driving a car or while you are in a situation that requires your complete attention ... *and* you should first discuss them with your doctor before you begin.)

Carolyn Gieger, a Qualified Yoga Teacher at the Hunterdon Health and Wellness Center in Whitehouse Station, New Jersey, has reviewed the following procedures, which also include some of her comments and recommendations.

Procedure I: Conscious Breathing

"A thing of beauty is a joy forever:
Its loveliness increases; it will never
Pass into nothingness; but still will keep
A bower quiet for us, and a sleep
Full of sweet dreams, and health, and quiet breathing."

John Keats, 1795-1821,
from "Endymion", a narrative poem,
Book 1, line 1

The Greek youth, **Endymion,** was granted eternal youth, sweet dreams, health and quiet breathing by **Selene,** the goddess of the moon. If *you* are similarly blessed by a Greek god (not a goddess since you are a woman) you may skip the suggestions in this chapter for *he* will have given you all you need for *Contentment.*

However, we mortals, who can't communicate on our cell phones with those heavenly creatures, will have to resort to practicing exercises to overcome the symptoms of stress. A good place to begin is exploring and reaping the benefits of *conscious breathing* procedures in contrast to chest breathing, which most of us do. There are several conscious breathing procedures. The most commonly recommended are *abdominal breathing* and *bellows breathing.* The exercises for abdominal breathing are covered here. References for details on bellows breathing, more rigorous, yoga-type techniques and others can be found in CHAPTER 21.

Abdominal Breathing

Remember the times when you were upset and tense because you were in a confrontation or were faced with an insoluble problem and you felt you were about to explode? Someone close to you ... your mother, father, husband or a friend ... said, "Slow down and take a deep breath." You did, and you felt so much better and were ready to handle the challenge. That's what conscious breathing is all about.

To benefit from *conscious breathing,* you don't have to read the next paragraph but you may skip to the exercises that follow. However, reading it may help you to understand how your body relaxes and reacts when you take deep, conscious breaths.

The act of breathing is the only bodily function that is both voluntary

60

and involuntary. The rapid, shallow breaths of *chest breathing* (involuntary) do not bring in large amounts of oxygen to our blood and thus fewer nutrients are delivered to our body tissues. *Abdominal breathing* (voluntary), also called diaphragmatic breathing, influences the nervous system, which regulates body functions we ordinarily can't control: blood pressure, heart rate, circulation, digestion and other bodily functions. The diaphragm is the large muscle between the chest and the abdomen. Deep breathing causes it to contract, forcing it downward and making the abdomen expand. Negative pressure forms in your chest and forces air into the lungs. Your lung air pockets expand, increasing your flow of blood and lymph (which is rich in immune cells), preventing infection of your lungs and other tissues. More importantly, you will feel relaxed and experience an overall sense of well-being because the breathing *with awareness* lessens and may also eliminate your tenseness and stress.

To learn if you are a chest or abdomen breather,
place your right hand on your chest, your left on your abdomen.
Breathe. Chest breathers' hands rise more.
The hand of the abdomen breather rises the greatest.
Don't be concerned if you are a chest breather;
you can easily learn to be a conscious breather.

The exercises for abdominal breathing

Yoga is a "breathing exercise" in which all physical movements begin with the breath … inhaling and exhaling. Learning the practices can be challenging, at first. However, Carolyn Geiger suggests that with patience and constant practice your movements can become fluid and rhythmic. She also recommends working with a Qualified Yoga Teacher, if not regularly, at least to get you started on your regimen.

You should allow five to ten minutes for each session of the following steps and perform them at least once every day. You will achieve even better results if you do them twice daily.

Step 1. Relax and sit comfortably on the floor in a cross-legged position or in a straight-back chair, your spine as upright as possible. Place your hands in your lap, palms facing up or down.

Step 2. Your eyes may be open or closed. If you keep them open,

61

concentrate on an object such as a candle, a flower, a doorknob, a lamp ... something that does not move, to help you develop a deep sense of focus. If you close your eyes, you may course to the "third eye center," the point between the eyebrows. Allow your mind to quiet and rid yourself of the pressing issues and concerns in your life. Focus on the moment and become conscious of your breathing.

Step 3. Begin by deeply drawing in your breath evenly through both nostrils. This makes your diaphragm pull air into the bottom of your lungs and inflate and expand your abdomen. Pause for a moment at the top of the inhale.

Step 4. Now exhale evenly, again, through both nostrils, feeling your abdomen pull in, then pause at the end of the exhale. Your breaths should be even in length, about four counts for the inhale and four for the exhale, until you become proficient with the lengths. Then you may lengthen the exhales.

Step. 5. Repeat the steps five times.

This breathing technique will help calm your mind and body. After you have practiced the exercises several times and have conquered the basic principles, you may add a bit of levity to your session by saying words to yourself that express the emotions you feel as you inhale and exhale ... such as *contentment, relaxation, peace, beauty* or any positive word or thought for inhaling, and *stress, anxiety, pain, grrrr* or other negative words for exhaling.

Procedure II: Relaxation Postures

Whereas *conscious breathing* keeps you in touch with your body functions, *relaxation postures* are designed to help you to *consciously relax* and keep you in touch with your entire body. Postures are *not* physical exercises, though you must exert yourself to move into them. They are stances into which you maneuver to make the body supple and flexible and to induce relaxation. The movements unify your body with your mind, your breath and your nervous system.

Most postures are derived from the ancient traditions of yoga with origins in Taoism, Islam, Buddhism and Hinduism and are known as ashtanga yoga, Anusara, Iyengar, viniyoga and others. However, many postures are similar in each style. The poses are countless. All take patience and perseverance to continue to perform. But the results are worth the effort for they will improve several areas of your health, help control your stress and prepare you for the practice of *meditation.*

Postures fall into several categories. Among them are:

Warm up	Seated	Inversions	Forward bends
Standing	Twist	Balance	Savasana

Within each category there can be scores more postures. Generally, the name of each pose describes that pose. Among the most commonly practiced are:

Easy Ground Work – Hatha Yoga Flow 1

The Child's Pose or Balasana

Animal postures:

Crocodile – Nakrasana

The Cat Cow Stretch

The Downward Dog – Adho Mukha Svanasana

The Cobra

The Triangle

The Butterfly Mudra

The Plough

The Tree

The Warrior

The Corpse Pose or Savasana, usually the last pose

In this chapter, starting below, I include instructions on how to prepare for "Do-It-Yourself Postures" and the how-to steps for the three most practiced postures: *the Sun Salutation /Salute to the Sun Pose, the Child's Pose and the Corpse Pose.* In CHAPTER 21 there are references for where you will find instructions not only for the postures I've listed but for many more and details about their benefits.

Practicing relaxation postures on your own can be a rewarding but daunting undertaking. You may choose, instead, to find a Qualified Yoga Teacher … there is at least one in most communities. You may enroll in a class at a studio or have private sessions with your own trainer/teacher. *Nothing can take the place of a Qualified Yoga Teacher, a professional who will help you perform postures correctly and avoid injury.* Once you have learned the basics you may then continue them on your own. Whichever route you take, *check with your doctor first* to make sure your body is in sound physical condition to permit you to handle the routines safely.

Preparing for "Do-It-Yourself Postures"

If you choose to carry out the poses at home using written instructions to guide you, there are several details that you should consider before you start:

1. Select a room or corner that is clean, uncluttered, quiet and filled with fresh air through a window that is slightly opened. Avoid distractions such as television and phones.

2. Wear loosely fitting, comfortable, breathable clothing and perform the postures in bare feet.

3. Place a yoga mat or several large, cushy terrycloth towels on the floor.

4. Do not eat a large meal for at least two hours before your session.

5. Have a blanket, sweater and socks handy in case you feel a chill.

6. Read and reread the instructions before you start each posture. Since it is difficult to read the instructions as you practice, you may consider taping them and listening to your recording as you perform the pose.

7. You may want to create a mood in your "Posture Area" by playing DVDs of soothing sounds like water rushing in a stream, wind rustling through leaves, a favorite melody ... whatever will help you relax..

Now you should be ready to begin your *Relaxation Postures*:
*Between each posture, pause, take a deep breath
and rest for a few moments before you proceed to the next.*

Sun Salutation

The Salute to the Sun Pose – Surya Namaskara

This set of asanas (poses) offers you a good cardiovascular workout and is an excellent way to keep physically fit. These postures help you keep your body in shape and your mind healthy and calm.

1. *Samasthiti:* Begin with the Prayer Pose. Keep your feet together and balance your weight equally on both feet. Expand your chest and relax your shoulders. As you breathe in, lift both arms up from your sides. As you exhale, bring your palms together in front of your chest in prayer position.

2. *Eka Inhale:* Raised Arm Pose. Breathing in, lift your arms up high with palms together.

3. *Due Exhale:* Hand to Foot Pose. Breathing out, bend forward until your hands touch your feet.

4. *Trini Inhale:* Look halfway up.

5. *Chatuari Exale:* Stick Pose. Jump up. Lie down on the floor, bring your whole body into a straight line.

6. *Pancha Inhale:* Cobra Pose. Stretch forward. Raise your chest and keep your arms straight.

7. *Shat Exhale, 5 Breaths:* Mountain Pose. Breathing out, lift your hips and tail bone, keeping chest down in an inverted V posture.

8. *Sapta Inhale:* Straighten legs. Bring your hands back to your toes and your head up.

9. *Ashtau Exhale:* Hand to Foot Pose. Breathing out, keep legs straight and your head at your knees.

10. *Nava Inhale:* Raised Arm Pose. Breathing in, roll the spine up and move your hands over your head.

11. *Tadasana Exhale:* As you exhale, straighten your body, then bring your arms down. Relax in this position and enjoy the calming sensations in your body.

The Child's Pose – Balasana

Balasana is a soothing posture that relieves the tension in the lower back and neck and the tightness in your shoulder blades. This pose is calming and stretches the legs, ankles, thighs, hips, knees and back muscles.

Your first step: Start by sitting upright on your knees, keeping them wide apart, your feet together, big toes touching, your fanny resting on your heels and your palms down.

Step 2. Breathe, inhaling deeply. While exhaling, bring your chest down between your knees and swing your arms forward in front of you and place your forehead on the mat.

Step 3. Bring your arms back to your sides and rest your hands, palms up, on either side of your feet.

Step 4. Take four deep, conscious breaths as you hold the *Child's Pose.*

Step 5. Return to the upright kneeling position with your back straight and your hands on your thighs.

Step 6. Repeat this pose two or three times.

The Corpse Pose – Savasana

Savasana is often considered the most difficult posture though it appears to be the most relaxing. Contradictorily, some instructors recommend this posture be practiced at the beginning of a session, others suggest the end and still others say it should be repeated several times during a session. You will find the *Corpse Pose,* which is one of total relaxation, may relieve your stress more quickly and completely than any others. *Savasana* will slow your heart and pulse rates and relax your complete psycho-physiological system.

Your first step: Lie flat on your back, with your arms stretched out comfortably at your sides, your palms facing up. Your legs should be slightly apart, your ankles and feet turned outward.

Step 2. Close your eyes. Be aware of your body, let it fall gently onto the mat. Start with the top of your head, go to your brow, drop your chin. Loosen your chest, your shoulders, your back, your pelvis, your legs … continue all the way down to your toes.

Step 3. Is your entire body completely at rest? Do you need a pillow anywhere to make you more comfortable? Be conscious of your natural breathing (don't alter it) and how relaxed you are. Let your mind travel to and linger on every part of your body from your forehead, to your eyes, nose, neck, to your fingertips and down to the tip of your toes.

Step 4. Once you experience complete relaxation, continue this pose of deep consciousness for five to ten minutes … as long as you wish.

Now, you are ready to Meditate!

Procedure III: Meditation

"They who have steeped their souls in meditation (prayer) can every anguish calmly bear."

Richard Monckton Milnes,
1801-1885, author

What is meditation?

Meditation is the act of training and emptying your mind by focusing on one sound, one word, one object or one thought to free it of all stress and distractions. You become more aware and conscious of your *self* by slowing down the sense of time passing. You learn to control your moods and thoughts before you are overwhelmed by stress and your psyche is dragged down even further into desperation.

The benefits of meditation

Meditation goes beyond lessening or eliminating stress. It has been known to improve one's health … the practice can lower blood pressure and heart and pulse rates; relieve insomnia; balance your physical, emotional and mental state, and lower the body's core temperature, which tends to extend your life. Your mind will be more alert, your reactions quicker and your understanding greater.

The Steps Toward Achieving Peace Through Meditation

Your first step: The place. Since the place where you meditate is as important as the procedure itself, a special section follows on *Creating Your Place for Meditation – Your Place of Peace.*

67

Step 2. Sit poised and alert, in a comfortable chair with your back erect and relaxed, but by no means rigid. Eastern cross-legged postures (half-lotus, full lotus, Burmese and Egyptian are difficult and often painful) are included in yoga references in CHAPTER 21. You should avoid a reclining position on a sofa or bed unless you do not tend to fall asleep if you rest during the day. You may have a pillow for your back to make you more comfortable and a throw handy if you get a chill.

Step 3. Select a time of day (early morning is best) and length of time for each session when there are no distractions. Plan your session the same time every day.

Step 4. Close your eyes.

Step 5. Select a word, phrase or thought to focus on, such as *love, peace, home, Springtime in Paris* ... whatever has a serene meaning for you. **Dr. Herbert Benson,** a professor and founding president of Mind/Body Medical Institute at Harvard Medical School, suggests if you select a *mantra* that focuses on a spiritual word, you will "achieve deep healing changes within your body and mind."

Step 6. Consciously relax every part of your body from the top of your head to your toes. Start with your forehead as you breathe in. Begin to let go of the tension in your body and the stress in your mind as you breathe out. Slowly, go down ... always breathing gently ... to your eyes, your nose, your mouth, your chin, your neck, your shoulders, your arms, your hands and fingers, your chest, your upper, middle and lower back, your stomach, your pelvis, your fanny, your thighs, your calves, your feet and finally your toes. Never stop focusing on *the object or mantra* you've chosen. Return your thoughts slowly up your body to the top or your head. Repeat ... down and back up.

Step 7. Breathe naturally, maintaining a passive attitude and ignore or set aside any intrusive sounds or thoughts. Make them go away.

Step 8. Continue for ten to fifteen minutes.

You may open your eyes to check the time but do not set the alarm. When you have finished your session, you may open your eyes, wait a minute or two before you stand. Rocking back and forth on your feet for a moment will help you get going and move on to the business of your day.

If, at first, you don't experience the peace you expect,
don't give up. It may take two or three sessions ...
to assure deep restfulness and serenity.
Just make sure you always maintain a passive attitude.

Creating your place for meditation – your place of peace

Where and when you choose to meditate is as critical to achieving the relaxation you seek as the meditation itself. The elements to consider for *Your Place:* the size, the location and the objects with which you surround yourself will create the ambience that will help you relax and separate you from the pressing concerns of having lost your loved one and handle the daunting tasks you must face.

The place, itself, can be any size ... a tiny corner in your bedroom, a nook in the kitchen, even a closet or a whole room if you have the space. But it should be private, quiet with no distractions and your very own retreat. (Later, you may find a few minutes throughout your day when you are alone ... riding the bus, train or airplane, waiting for an appointment ... that you may dedicate to meditating.)

The *objects* you select for *Your Place* should be intimate, memorable, relate to tranquility and have special meaning within themselves and/or for you. You don't need to have them all as I suggest below, but choose as many as you wish to make you feel comfortable, serene and prepared to meditate.

1. Start with a small table or low shelf on which you place a colorful scarf directly or in a tray or on a mat. You may enjoy looking for and finding a puja cloth to use ... it is a two-sided, printed silk runner that is used during a Hindu ritual.

2. In the center of your cloth, place a candle in a votive holder (to avoid a fire) and away from flammable materials. You may select your candle by color since color has symbolic significance: blue for healing negative emotions; white for peace; violet or indigo for spirituality; green for your body and mind; orange for energy, and yellow for joy and happiness.

69

3. Surround your candle with familiar objects: flowers, each variety also has significance; a favorite book; a typed quotation; a photograph; a small painting; a statue or a figurine; a small water fountain; whatever is soothing and will help you relax.

4. Filling *Your Place* with a fresh scent of flowers, herbs, fruit or mint will help prepare the ambience for meditation. Back in the 1930s **Dr. Edward Bach,** an English physician, developed flower essences to help the healing process. You can select from among these essences:

   Arnica treats your trauma
   Sage contributes to your wisdom
   Lavender calms you
   Impatiens helps you accept
   Peppermint and spearmint cool and invigorate you
   Lemongrass lifts your spirits
   Sandalwood soothes your mind

All you need to reap the benefits of the scent you choose are a few drops of the oil in a cup of very hot water which will diffuse and fill *Your Place* with a steaming, soothing fragrance. Another option is to burn incense.

You may choose to have another smaller *place* as well, in your kitchen, where we all spend so much of our time. You may have just a candle that you light when you're there in the morning to remind you that "the beauty of the world has two edges, one of laughter and one of anguish," and you have chosen laughter.

Are you ready to make your stress melt away?

You don't have to practice *all* the procedures I've included to launch your stress management program and keep in touch with your emotions. You may begin with one procedure or just a few steps of another ... those you feel most comfortable with and don't take too much of your time. You should, however, set a schedule and practice at least a few minutes each day. Perform the few you've chosen, repeat them and increase them. You may find you will want to do more until you have completed an entire procedure. Perhaps you will, then, go on to another until you've conquered all three. Don't give up! You may even want to go further and check CHAPTER 21 for where you can get more information and expand one or more of the processes.

Remember the double caveat: Check with your doctor
before performing the breathing and posture procedures.
And don't meditate while driving a car or
when you are in a situation that requires your complete attention.
If you meditate in a bus or on a train,
make sure you are alert enough to get off at your destination.

CHAPTER 8

Be Kind to Me Day

*I*n the early days of my career, when I was a fashion editor at *Woman's Day* magazine one of my colleagues, **Nancy,** came into the office looking fresher and more vibrant than usual. I was curious since she had a trying day ahead of her working at a photo shoot with our *The Devil Wears Prada*-type boss. She must have sensed my surprise. "Oh," she said with a lilt in her voice, "Yesterday was my 'Be Kind to Nancy Day.' I'm ready for whatever the 'Witch of Seventh Avenue' dishes out."

With all due respect to her, **MPG,** *The* Fashion Editor, was a brilliant, informed style maven who knew how to spot and promote the best classic fashion trends. She would swish in and out of showrooms with her veiled-pill box hat on top of her head (right for the era) and her long black silk cape billowing behind her. She would order designers around, abruptly turning down clothes or graciously accepting those she chose to feature in the magazine.

MPG was a hard-driving, no-nonsense woman. She had her hang ups and did not hesitate to take them out on her staff, including me. This she would do to the embarrassment of the photographers and models, who would slink into the background to escape her harangues. Nevertheless, I owe much to her ... I learned about design, style and the whims of the fashion world. She taught me how to trust my instincts. She would ask for my opinion, subtly crediting me for good taste, which I never realized I had.

But that day, it was from Nancy that I learned a more important lesson that was to help me countless times afterwards. She told me how she prepared for the anticipated session of verbal abuse (and how she managed other difficult situations) ... she pampered herself for several hours. It was Sunday, the day before ... she rose late, took a hot bubble bath, gave herself a pedicure, indulged in a breakfast that included strawberries and whipped cream with several cups of hot coffee, dressed in jeans and T-shirt and took a walk in Central Park with her puppy, came home, locked herself in her room and read a romance novel.

She was ready!

Since then, I pamper myself whenever I need and deserve a respite, particularly when the loss of my husband overwhelms me. I've made my own list of indulgences for my "Be Kind to Victoria Days" and I add more from time to time. For this book, I have interviewed single-again women and professionals and have found other special pleasures for you to practice during your *"Be Kind to Me Day."*

Try it, you'll love it!

You deserve to pamper yourself with whatever whim gives you the bounce-back you need. There are endless options to delight in. I list some here. You may have others you've always wanted to do but did not take the time to explore or felt guilty to even consider. Do them! You're entitled.

Design your own *"Be Kind to Me Day"* from this list of indulgences. It can be as long or as short as you want: for two or three hours before you go to work, a full morning, an afternoon, an extended two-hour lunch, an evening or a whole day. Even an hour will refresh you.

Start Your "Be Kind to Me Day"

Get up late, wash your face and don't apply make-up, climb into your tub with water as hot as you can stand, add a few drops of your favorite oil fragrance and soak until the water begins to cool or add hot if you want to stay longer.

Get out of the tub, cover your face and body with lotion and powder, throw on a baggy robe, lounge on a couch with a cup of coffee or tea (see the last page of this chapter) and choose your next indulgence.

Breakfast: Prepare the breakfast you always wanted but choose not to because of the calories. Eggs, toast, sausages, waffles, hash brown potatoes, pancakes, bacon, crepes. Name it! Have it!

Pamper your face and your body: Do it yourself or wallow in a session at a salon or a spa, see CHAPTER 9. Treat yourself to a massage, a facial, a shampoo with a blow-dry or a completely new style by your favorite hairdresser, and a manicure, which should include the most exciting current shade of polish. Don't neglect the relaxing pedicure (an RFM, a reflexology foot massage, again, see CHAPTER 9, making sure your toe nails match or dare to contrast your fingernails.

Pig out: Cook up a pot of spaghetti and serve it with your favorite sauce. Lunch at a fast-food place: McDonald's, Wendy's, Burger King. (Wear your sunglasses and casual clothes if you don't want your friends to catch you cheating on your diet.) How about some potato chips, nachos or that hot fudge sundae you crave with whipped cream, nuts and a maraschino cherry? Or dine on a gourmet dish at home or in a French, Greek, Italian, Thai or any other chic bistro.

Mangia!

Do an easy exercise: A walk in the park if you live in the city, a wooded trail if you have a home in the country. A few laps at your local "Y" pool or at a swim club where the eligible men hang out.

A shopping spree: Wear your flats so you'll be able to shop as long as your money holds out. Bring a pair of heels for trying on dressy clothes.

Practice some relaxation procedures: See CHAPTER 7: *Handling Stress.* Perform all or parts of the steps: conscious breathing ... relaxation postures ... meditation.

Diversions: Watch a soap opera during the day. Watch a prime-time sitcom (not the news, it's too disturbing) or a DVD from Netflix while sipping French wine from your finest goblet and snacking on French brie on thin slices of a crusty baguette. Call the local cultural center or theater and request last-minute, discounted tickets for the opera, ballet or a play. Attend the performance you've always wanted to see but have put off because "I don't have the time."

Call a close, understanding friend and talk as long as she/he will listen. *Volunteer* for an hour or two at a benefit or philanthropy of your choice. *Read* a good or trashy novel or flip through pages of the magazines you have accumulated for months in a hefty pile you've wanted to discard.

Have a private tea party, alone or with one or more good friends. Prepare a hot pot of herb tea or just add a dash of spice to a cup of the brand you usually drink. Take small sips, breathe in the aroma and enjoy the soothing and warming (or cooling) sensations. Teas do wonders for your health and you'll be pleasantly surprised to feel your spirits energized. Here are some teas to try:

Chamomile is mild and calming; *vanilla* is sweet and soothing; *cardamon* excites the mind; *peppermint* is relaxing and cooling; *ginger* is a stimulant that relieves body aches and nausea; *lemon* lessens tension and stress; *green,* an antioxidant, reduces chances of heart disease and other ailments, and *cloves* will give you that overall cozy, warm feeling. Adding a dash of *cinnamon* to any cup of tea will help your circulatory system and encourage other herbs and spices to carry out their wonders more quickly.

Now, you should be ready to create your own *"Ultimate Be Kind to Me Day"* and pamper yourself as often as you wish or need. Be selective … and choose the indulgences that are best for you. Of course, you won't try to do them all at one time.

Remember, if you can't spend a full day pampering yourself when you feel you should, get up early on an occasional morning and spend one or two hours indulging in the options that do the most for you. Or spend the hour or two at the end of the day when you come home from work or after any trying day. You deserve to be kind to yourself as often as you wish.

When you are in your state of euphoria,
you may put off your responsibilities but do <u>not</u> neglect them later.
Your "Be Kind to Me Day" is designed to enable you
to handle challenges, refreshed and restored …
with a clear mind and a healthy body.

CHAPTER 9

A Great New Look

"Looking good is the best revenge!"

This cliché is overused but not overrated. When you do everything possible to make sure you look great you are on your way to taking charge of your life and *Finding Solitary Contentment*.

Many years ago, when I was in my twenties, I came across a photo-feature in a fashion magazine that has had a lasting impression on me. The article was titled *"You can be more beautiful, at times, than a fashion model."* I was startled because I never considered myself particularly beautiful. I didn't have to be *as* beautiful. I'd settle for pretty or perhaps, *almost* as beautiful. There were two photos of the same model, one as she smiled, the other as she frowned. She appeared amazingly unattractive in the photo as she frowned! The writer suggested that the reader look in a mirror and do the same. When I smiled, *I* felt and looked pretty. I looked far better than the frowning model. I refused to frown! Since then, whenever I catch myself frowning, I smile.

So, *smile even if it hurts!* Smiling, when you are downcast, grieving or experiencing other negative emotions, can become a habit and is an easy, cost-free way to being truly beautiful. It can even take off a few years. I'm sure you've been told that you have a beautiful smile, *so smile.*

You've taken the first step in creating your *great new look* ... you're smiling! The act of smiling does more than enhance your "look," it will uplift you and give you inner peace, which is the wellspring for how you look to others and to yourself. *You will glow!* You'll be encouraged to take on the physical steps, many of which you will find in this chapter, designed to help you improve your overall appearance. These are more

77

difficult than smiling and you'll need to set aside time to carry them out. If you persevere you'll be rewarded with your great new look. You will be confident, unique, sensuous, irresistible and surprising!

In this chapter, you'll also find references
to other places and people
you may contact for answers to your own particular challenges.

Where Do You Start?

There are two phases to the *new look* program. Most women jump to the second without even realizing there is a first. I learned about the first, *the healing process* of "repair, restore, revive," from **Donna Zahn,** a licensed cosmetologist and a certified reflexologist. This phase sets the foundation for the second, *visible or outward cosmetics.* The first can assure lasting rewards from the second. Soon after I began Donna's healing process I experienced a greater sense of well-being. Now, as I repeat the steps with a regular regimen my well-being rarely falters. This phase is easier and more relaxing than the second because you put yourself in the hands of a professional who is dedicated to healing your body ... and as a result, your mind.

"Feeling great is even better!"

I The Healing Phase

The emotional stress of handling the loss of a loved one, along with the turmoil and demands that follow, take a dramatic toll on our bodies, our minds and our spirit. There are services available, says Donna, who is also a certified massage therapist, that will repair, restore and revive the feeling of wellness that is essential to our bodies and our spiritual health. These are not the "frivolous" spa-type services that attract celebrities, are expensive and boast about their facilities in expansive, glamorous resorts. They serve the purpose of those who have the means. To help *you* on your path to a healthy body and mind, you can try the Internet and Yellow Pages for professionals in your area for healing services you can afford. Suggestions that follow in this chapter will guide you.

However, if you want to splurge and mingle with the *swells,* (the elite), go for it!

A Facial: Though Donna recommends starting by treating yourself to a facial, I began with what I expected would be an old-fashioned pedicure ... she calls the treatment a *reflexology foot massage.* (See later in this chapter to learn what it did for me and can do for you. She convinced me that it is much more than a pedicure.) A proper facial will begin with an analysis of your skin type: dry, oily, combination or dehydrated. The treatment will help restore moisture to your skin, add suppleness, remove fine lines and create a well-rested appearance. You will not only feel the difference, your friends will notice and ask where you found the fountain of youth. Donna suggests repeating the facial two to three times a year.

There are caveats about treating your skin from **Dr. Leslie Baumann,** dermatologist at the Baumann Cosmetic & Research Institute in Miami Beach, Florida and author of *The New York Times* best-selling book, *The Skin Type Solution.* She cautions against using products with benzoyl peroxide and pricey anti-aging creams. As we get older, our skin dries and becomes thinner, and the benzoyl peroxide removes moisture. The creams can clog pores. Dr. Baumann recommends moisturizers with glycerin and ceramides to prevent drying and prescription-only creams with retinoids for wrinkles.

Body Massage: Caring for your body is often more important than what you do with your face. How you move is a dead giveaway on how old you appear. A quick step, sitting down and getting up with agility, bounding up stairs are all signs of a fit body and youthfulness. A regimen of exercise detailed in CHAPTER 6 will help keep you in shape.

Having a body massage can ease your way to taking on the rigid routine of exercise. You have to experience this treatment to enjoy the complete sense of well-being. Of course, you will feel wonderful. You are meant to. More importantly, massage is therapeutic and contributes to your overall health. It is not just for a sense of relaxation. Your muscles tightened by the stress of your loss will loosen, the pain will lessen and your circulation will increase ... all benefits for your body and your spirit.

What exactly is massage? Massage is the act of manipulating the body by a certified massage therapist with pressure, tension, motion or vibration done by hands or fingers. The parts of the body that are treated may include one or more of the following: muscles, tendons, ligaments, skin and connective joints.

Massage therapy is a treatment for ailments with various types of manipulation designed for each specific need. Sports, stretch therapy and deep-tissue massage to alleviate painful muscles, of course, are for athletes. For sinuses, migraines, cramps and overall body tension, there are several: aromatherapy, shiatsu, reiki, Swedish and more. Once you find the certified massage therapist you are comfortable with, he/she will help you determine which is the best for you.

Reflexology foot massage: This massage offers much more than the spa pedicure, which is, of course, relaxing, therapeutic and cosmetic because it gives us the "pretty feet" we all want. *RFM* is something unique, and far from a new technique. In fact, *reflexology* dates back more than four thousand years to when Egyptian slaves manipulated the feet of pharaohs and members of royal families as can be seen in wall paintings and hieroglyphics.

This practice of *reflexology* focuses on the two thousand meridians (nerve points) running vertically through your entire body, making it possible for the operator to finger any given point easily. The results are therapeutic relief of more than stress of the back, shoulders and neck but a soothing of sinus problems, sore joints, insomnia, migraines and more. *All by having your feet manipulated!* According to Donna Zahn, who has been a certified massage therapist and practitioner of this method for a decade, "The sense of well-being and relaxation you experience after a session, lasts several days and you will feel fantastic!" Just as I did!

Home care for your feet: If you can't afford the *RFM* or prefer to take care of your tootsies yourself, the American Podiatric Medical Association has some helpful tips. They do not promise the sens-ational results of *RFM* but your soles will be soothed, you will have "happy feet" and you'll feel pampered.

1. Place a bucket (large enough for both your feet) of warm water in front of a comfortable chair.

2. You may sit, but before placing your feet in the water:

a. remove your nail polish with non-acetone remover.

b. begin stimulating and warming your feet by placing one at a time on your lap. Hold your foot and move your thumbs slowly from the top of your toes to the bottom of your heel. Repeat this process several times until your feet get warm and relaxed.

c. trim your toenails straight across. Using an emery board, file the edges.

3. Now you can take the plunge ... both feet into the warm water. Ooh! Aah! Let them soak for five or ten minutes. Dip a foot file or pumice stone in the water, raise one foot at a time and with the file or stone, using gentle strokes, smooth the dry skin on your heels and the balls and sides of your feet.

4. If you want to soothe and soften even more, massage your feet and your lower legs with a scrub.

5. You are on the last step to achieving your "happy feet." Using a clean towel, dry your feet and your toes. As you dry, you will be loosening your foot joints; with one hand, cup your heel and with the other, grab the top of your foot. Slowly, rotate the foot at the ankle a few times in each direction.

You're done! Admire and enjoy your "pretty feet!"

Another tip from a podiatrist I visited: Apply over-the-counter Eucerin to your soles and heels on a regular basis to keep them smooth and avoid dry and flaky skin. Eucerin may also be used on other parts of the body, hands, elbows and legs.

If you have the time and the wherewithall
Donna suggests having one of these treatments once a month.
Even having just one ... the one that does the most for you ...
every other month will contribute to your well-being.

II The Cosmetic Phase

Most of us know what we like least about our appearance. I have fine, hard-to-manage hair, a full face, wide hips and a tummy that's not as flat at it used to be. But, everyone tells me I still have great legs and good skin. *I agree with them!* Minimizing my negatives has been hard work. Maintaining my assets, even harder, but it's been worth it. I'm pleased that I finally reached my best look, for now. I'm still not beautiful but for my years I'm close. However, as new products and trendy styles *that suit me* come on the market, I might update my look.

Do It Yourself: A good way to begin is by *taking an inventory* (another list) of your best features, those that are less than your best and those you want to improve or change completely. Stand in front of a mirror (full-length if you have one) and scrutinize. Be as honest as you can and analyze what you should do and proceed on your own. You may begin with your face, or skip to the feature that concerns you most or those that need the most attention.

Experiment ... with make-up, with hairstyles, exercises for your body, a new wardrobe. *Rule No 1:* Draw attention to your best attributes. *Rule No 2:* Work hard on the ones that can be changed for the better.

The Professional Route: This is the easier, quicker, more reliable way to go.

Your face: According to Donna Zahn, properly selected and applied cosmetics will enhance any woman's inner and outer beauty. If you are not familiar with all the latest cosmetics and their uses, she recommends seeking the advice of a make-up consultant in a salon ... but this may be a little pricey. Instead, you may find a high-end retail store, such as Sephora, Macy's, Neiman Marcus and Nordstrom, that have formal make-up counters with consultations, evaluations and applications available at no charge except for a minimal purchase of a product. You will be treated to a consultation and an evaluation. The technician will analyze your face, your age, your skin tone and guide you to the moisturizer, make-up and colors that are right for you. She'll help you apply them for the final result which will perfect your look and please you.

Your hair: Here again, Donna, and this time she *firmly* suggests you seek advice at a professional salon for hairstyling and coloring. Shop around for the salon with an ambience and staff that you will be comfortable with for a long time. The most expensive will not necessarily give you what you are looking for. Your best bet is a stylist/

colorist who consults with you to learn your lifestyle: a professional business woman, a stay at home, a social butterfly, a gardener, a single who needs uplifting ... whatever you are or choose to be. She offers suggestions for a new style based on the shape of your face and the color that will best complement your skin, your age and the color of your eyes. You should also determine the amount of time and money you want to or are able to spend each month on maintaining your style and color. Keep looking, you may find someone who not only makes you beautiful but who may become a friend and even a confidant. It happens and it may, happily, happen to you!

Permanent cosmetics/micropigmentation

Micropigmentation is a topical (skin) procedure that creates *permanent* cosmetic effects through the use of needles. You may select the shape and color you wish for your lips, eyebrows and other areas to enhance your features. On the other hand, plastic surgery is a true surgical procedure that reshapes or reconstructs the face, breasts or other parts of the body to or from the original form.

This micropigmentation service, according to Donna, should only be done by a certified permanent cosmetics professional who is a member of the American Academy of Micropigmentation and has liability insurance. She recommends, *always,* ask to see documented certification and the school diploma of the technician before you commit to proceed. Checking with others who have used the services performed by your selected professional will also assure you that you have made the right choice.

The process of micropigmentation is used by women who suffer from alopecia (loss of hair caused either by stress or following chemotherapy) or by mastectomy patients who need areola replacement after reconstructive surgery. The application of varying degrees of color and shadows creates an illusion of the original areola. This process must be conducted under the direct supervision of a doctor, most often by the surgeon who performed the breast reconstruction. Patients usually describe the results as "wonderful."

However, if you are a baby boomer in your fifties (more or less), you may consider this procedure if your eyebrows are thinning; your eyesight has dimmed and you have difficulty applying make-up or you have become allergic to cosmetics. Others who find the procedure helpful are women who have little time to apply their make-up as often as they would like: women who exercise often, travel extensively and those who have cosmetic allergies. You may choose to have your eyebrows defined and eyeliners, lip liners or lip shading applied permanently. You will be happy with amazingly satisfying results.

The procedure is conducted in a clean, sterile environment and does have, as any that involves breaking the skin, some discomfort, but it is bearable. The technician uses a machine with needles of various sizes as necessary for the skin's thickness and to finish the area being treated. Topical anesthetics and creams are applied to lessen any unpleasant sensation during the procedure. Some swelling may occur but will last for only a day to a day and a half. If you follow the pre- and after-treatment instructions you will experience minimal discomfort and will be delighted with your long-lasting new look. But be sure you adhere to the admonitions of no drinking, no drugs and no smoking before and for some time after your session.

Plastic surgery

Surgical procedures can contribute positively to your *Great New Look* and to your self-image as well. Even a small difference can be uplifting. There are two upfront caveats: First, since the changes are permanent and often dramatic, you should understand how your emotional well-being may be affected. *Second,* you should delay any decision until the grieving for the loss of your loved one or other crises are far behind you. Once you feel you are ready, consider the following questions:

Do I *want* to have plastic surgery?

Or do I *need* plastic surgery?

Your answer can be a quick way to determine whether you should undertake this procedure now or reconsider and delay your decision to another time.

If you *want* the surgery, according to professional counselor **Beverly Zagofsky,** you may be ready to proceed. No matter which response you give, you must spend time in consultation and evaluation.

However, if you feel you *need* the procedure, you may require a great deal of soul-searching and seek further professional counseling.

The Want Candidate: You have been honest with yourself and know exactly why you have chosen to have plastic surgery. You may be alone but you have regained your self-confidence, you have an area of your face or body that has changed over the years that you wish to improve and you expect *realistic* results. Or you have a defect or flaw that you've had for sometime and now you want to eliminate. You are ready to "go for it."

The Need Candidate: You are showing your age and you wish to recapture your youth and restore your former lifestyle with a partner. You need a major new appearance, a new nose or body image to change your life completely. If these are your wishes, you have unrealistic expectations and will never be satisfied. You should take time, lots of it, seek professional help and lower your expectations.

Choosing a surgeon: It is paramount that you select a qualified surgeon whom you trust and with whom you are comfortable. You may ask your family doctor for a recommendation. Or visit the online referral service of the American Society of Plastic Surgeons (ASPS). Surgeons who are ASPS members have five years of surgical training with at least two in plastic surgery; are trained in all plastic surgery procedures; operate in accredited medical facilities; adhere to a strict code of ethics, and continue to fill medical education requirements, including standards and innovations in patient safety.

Available surgeries: Most plastic surgeons offer the following procedures and will help you determine what is right for you and how to fulfill your needs:

Facelift	Facial implants	Breast lift
Eyelid surgery	Injectable fillers	Tummy tuck
Nose surgery	Skin resurfacing	Spider veins
Brow lift	Breast augmentation	Liposuction
	Body contouring	

Injectable fillers

Injectable fillers will enhance different parts of your face and are usually performed as outpatient procedures by a plastic surgeon or a qualified physician. Injectables are designed to fill in wrinkles and fine lines, depress scars, eliminate crow's feet, banish neck bands and enlarge lips. Results for the most part are immediate, will last from two to six months and the treatment may be repeated.

Botox is the best known and most widely performed injectable filler procedure available among seven selections. At the time of this writing, three have been approved by the Federal Drug Administration: *Botox (Botulinum Toxin Type A), Artefill and Restylane (produced in Sweden).* The others are *Juvéderm, Perlane, Radiesse* and *Sculptura.* It is essential that you discuss the procedure with a physician who is certified to administer injectable fillers to learn if you are a qualified patient and which filler will produce the results you wish.

Ultherapy

Cosmetic dermatologist **Dr. Leslie Baumann** suggests considering *Ultherapy,* a procedure that uses the body's own regenerative response to delicately and steadily restore memory to the skin and the underlying tissue. As with other ultrasound procedures, an applicator placed on the skin projects an image onto a screen that allows the practitioner to plan where the energy will be directed. The applicator is then used to deliver low levels of heat at the right depth below the skin to achieve a positive effect. The skin's response to the energy is to arouse the growth of new collagen. A gradual tightening occurs, resulting in a natural lift of the skin over time. Comfort levels vary from a sensation of brief prickling to heat beneath the skin.

If you choose to undertake a medical procedure
be sure you are ready ... emotionally and physically ...
that you have taken all the necessary steps
to prepare for the surgery/treatment,
the temporary discomfort and the recovery period.

III Your Style

When you begin to analyze your style, you don't need to empty your closets and drawers and replace your entire wardrobe to achieve your *Great New Look*. Once you've defined a style that's right for you, go through your clothes and accessories and set aside those that will complement the new pieces you'll purchase. Getting rid of the rest that you haven't worn for a year or two and no longer want to wear is a good start!

Your total best, current style is made up of several parts which when blended together, create a chic whole. Besides, it is a good idea to be aware of the do's and don'ts of those parts, particularly for those of us who are close to fifty or more. They are worth doing and don'ting even if you already look years younger than you are.

Don'ts

1. *First and foremost: Don't* dress as though you are twenty nor over the hill, and *don't wear*:

2. trendy outfits unless they flatter your figure

3. tight-fitting clothes, except swimsuits

4. horizontal stripes

5. large-patterned pants

6. cropped jackets or those that hit mid thigh

7. uncomfortable shoes

8. pleated pants

9. low-rise jeans

10. the wrong thing to the right place

Do's:

1. Define your style and be a little, but not too, racy

2. If your tummy or fanny is large, wear solid colors, especially in pants

3. If your hips are broad, flat-front pants or a dark, slim pencil skirt with matching hose will do great things for your figure and your confidence

4. Wear clothes that fit your lifestyle

5. Use accessories, scarves, jewelry or belts to change any basic outfit

6. Try spare separates; crisp white blouses and smart, skirt suits

7. If you can splurge, try a new, trendy handbag that will go with anything and make a statement about you

8. Stand in front of a full length mirror and *experiment* until you find your best style

You may call on a good friend, a daughter or another close relative to help you define a style that's current and right for you. If you are ready to shop, decide on the items you want. On a budget? You'll find great selections in stores like Target and Marshall and discount outlets that carry designer clothes at affordable prices. Or check the upscale department stores and local boutiques. Their clothing and accessories departments often have stylist-salespeople with excellent taste who are happy to help you purchase fashions that complement your figure and coloring.

Professional help

There are *Image Makers* you can call on if you really want and can afford to splurge. You may need a lot of help or you especially want to look your best as you try to get back into the job market or change jobs.

Sharon Kornstein is founder and president of ImageDesign, a full-service and image consultation company that helps develop "an effective visual image for professionally minded men and women by blending their physical characteristics, personal preferences and industry requirements into a unique, comfortable and cohesive style." Ms Kornstein notes that an image-maker offers advice that creates a new style/image for women that assures a great look and gives them greater confidence. During one-on-one consultations, you receive suggestions for flattering clothing and accessory styles; colors; hair styling; eyeglasses, and make-up that bring out your best features, as well as tips on how to organize your wardrobe. There are personal shopping trips with your consultant that save you time and money and give you a feeling of being in control, not only of your wardrobe and how you look, but of your overall image.

You may have to stretch your budget but the image-maker service just may create the *Great New Look* you are seeking ... and in the long run it will be worth the investment.

Don't try to make all your changes at once.
Perfect each feature before going on to the next.
However, start your exercise regimen today and repeat it every day.
You'll be on your way to your Great New Look and Solitary Contentment.
And maybe a new guy, if that's what you wish!

CHAPTER 10

Face Your Sexuality Head On

"Experience is sexy!"

says fifty-two- year-old actress
Kristin Scott Thomas,
the paragon of cool, reserved English
beauty and star of "Four Weddings and
a Funeral" and "The English Patient"

*Y*ou have been there!

You've had a rewarding relationship for years *(or was it less than rewarding?)* in or out of wedlock … your sex life was good, adequate or even great and now your partner is gone. You may have wandered on occasion, but mostly you were true. You have experienced sex. Now that you are alone, you wonder: Are you *sexy?* You lie in bed alone at night remembering … touching, kissing, loving and sex seemed so easy and natural when you were young … younger. You are older, much older now … does the desire diminish? Will you ever have sex again? Do you want to replace the lover you lost? Is there a partner out there for you? Or would you just as soon be alone?

What is sex at your age, anyway? What *is* sex at any age? What does sex mean to you … how do you define sex? We each have our own definition of sex based on our experience, dreams and fantasies. At this stage in your life, is it proper to fantasize or even think about sex? Are your feelings normal, acceptable? How much *do* you care? Or do you care at all? If you are reading this chapter, you care, even a little.

You are not alone when you question and muse about your sexuality and desperately miss the one who is no longer there for you. Most, if not all widows, divorcées and the betrayed have similar doubts.

91

When my husband died of Parkinson's disease, I had no questions about sex or my sexuality. I was in denial. Complete denial. I had no interest in men, any man, let alone sex. I was repelled even by the thought of an encounter. I felt guilty when a rare fantasy crept into my mind. If Kevin Costner, Bruce Willis, Robert Duvall or any other mature sex symbol came calling, I would have turned him away. What I needed was peace and spiritual comfort. I returned to church for the first time in years as I had planned when I learned that Ralph's illness would take him from me.

During the coffee hour on my first Sunday back to church, **Carolyn,** a lovely, mature blonde approached me. She immediately sensed my need, for she, too, was a widow and had lost her husband Karl to Parkinson's as well, four years earlier. She suggested we have lunch. Later that week, we met at the small town's café where in the privacy of a quiet booth Carolyn shared memories of her life with Karl, his career as a Washington, D.C. lobbyist, their busy social life and the years she cared for him before he succumbed. It was all very familiar and heartbreaking. Now she was living a full life volunteering as a greeter at the church and holding a part-time job as a sales clerk in the designer boutique a few stores from where we were lunching. I felt comfortable and at ease knowing that someone related to my grief and I told her about my life with Ralph and my loss. The conversation was gratifying for us both.

As we sipped our second cups of tea, Carolyn launched into what was unfamiliar territory for me. She talked in detail about the widows and divorcées she knew and the men in their lives ... *and* hers. Naïve me! Lonely women. Vulnerable women. She learned about their exploits from one of her close gay friends, a physician. Among them was a "dirty old man" who came to him for a prescription for Viagra. He wanted it for the first date with a widow he was meeting for dinner that night. Then Carolyn went on about her current relationship with a wealthy "man about town" who had been a member of the same circle she shared with her husband. John was her lover as well as that of another woman. *They shared him!* (But not at the same time.) "There are *not* many men of our age around who are appealing, come without baggage," she said, "and with whom you would want to sleep. John and I have many interests and friends in common. We have good times together." Stunned, I replied, "I'm not interested in another man and not at all in sex." "Oh," she declared, "I enjoy sex! It is wonderful to have someone want you, touch you and make love to you."

Though what Carolyn told me was disturbing, I know she meant well and hoped to prepare me for what to expect. I was far from ready! It took more than six months for me to understand that you may experience a hiatus in wanting or being able to engage in sex again. Then, after the shock of your loss grows less, you may once again become aware of your body and your desires. You may be surprised to find that the inclination can return despite any roadblocks you encounter as you recover from the loss of your lover.

As you ponder, remind yourself: "Experience is sexy!"

There are women doctors (and some who are men) ... family and sex therapists, researchers and teachers ... who understand and relate to your needs. They are dedicated to sharing their findings, knowledge and experience to help women face their sexuality. They publish articles and books. They lecture, serve on panels, conduct group therapy sessions and give advice on radio and television programs. (I list some in CHAPTER 21.)

Dr. Gina Ogden, a marriage, family and sex therapist, teacher and researcher, has authored several books with concepts that break away from old beliefs and unite sex with the body, mind, heart and spirit. In her book, *The Heart and Soul of Sex,* she sets forth encouraging tenets that she labels *Desiderata,* or "things you desire." These ten rights for women are designed to help you begin to see your way through your sexual dilemmas and go on to help you overcome them.

Desiderata: Your Right to Intimacy and Pleasure

1. I have a right to my own body and all of its sensations, including pleasure and pain.

2. I have a right to think my own thoughts, whatever they may be.

3. I have a right to feel the full range of my emotions – excitement, joy and anger, sorrow and depression, love and fear – whether or not my feeling them is acceptable to others.

4. I have a right to acknowledge my memories, whether they are memories of delight or abuse, and to base present relationship decisions on them.

5. I have a right to be – or not to be – a sexual person at all ages and stages of my life, and a right to choose how I define what I mean by sexuality.

6. I have a right to expect my partner to respect my body, thoughts, feelings, and general well-being, and a right to insist on respect, if necessary.

7. I have a right to ask for what I want.

8. I have a right to say no to any sexual encounter that feels unsatisfying or threatening – physically, emotionally, spiritually, or sexually.

9. I have a right to say yes to pleasure that is physically, emotionally, spiritually and sexually safe.

10. I have a right to feel good about saying yes and no to "things you desire."

Since the early days of the '50s when the Kinsey Reports revealed sexual behavior patterns to the world, there have been more polls conducted that have current answers to questions we raise. The study on "Sexuality in Midlife and Beyond" by Harvard Medical School, edited by **Dr. Alan Altman,** Assistant Clinical Professor, Harvard and certified sex therapist **Suki Hanfling** at the Institute for Sexuality and Intimacy in Belmont, Massachusetts, is one of the most recent. From a strictly biological perspective, they report, sex is "another hormone-driven bodily function designed to perpetuate the species." But both experts proceed to show that sex is far more complex than the physical, and encompasses a splendid panoply of emotions – tenderness, love, excitement, longing, disappointment and anxiety. And, as we mature and find ourselves without a partner, we question our sexuality.

The study defines sex as more than the so-called act of "genital-to-genital contact." There are pleasurable activities that include other parts of the body ... the mouth, the hands, the breasts and sensitive areas of the skin when caressed can create erotic sensations. You don't need a partner, they indicate, to enjoy sex. Watching films, fantasizing and masturbating are all acceptable methods of achieving sexual gratification.

These specialists have documented with well-researched answers sex-related problems for women, men and couples. They acknowledge the sex issues faced by women who have lost lovers: that we fear we'll not be aroused with a new partner; since we are older and our bodies have changed we may feel self-conscious naked in bed, or we're anxious because we may have forgotten how to perform. Unfortunately, though they realize that we have feelings of guilt, inadequacy and need, they do not offer specific remedies to overcome them. However, if you do need help they say that there is always a sex therapist in the wings to give you the self-assurance you seek.

The Women's Liberation Movement that was launched in the '60s has put a new spin on how we view and acknowledge sex. Two recent studies reveal some of the acts which today are relatively acceptable, phone sex, watching adult films, the use of sex toys and masturbation … in the past were never discussed, were believed practiced only by perverts and considered taboo. These reports, Harvard Medical School's "Sexuality in Midlife and Beyond" and AARP's "The Secret Lives of Single Women," by **Sarah Mahoney,** show that today's single woman is open to dealing with sex and can live with it or without it.

As you read some of the results, you may learn how you fit in among other mature, single women in your interests, needs and desires concerning your own sexuality. You may consider choosing to venture beyond the old-time taboos and enjoy sex more fully.

Among the forty-five-plus women in AARP's study, only 22% were sexually active during the past six months, and only 18% had a regular partner … however "they were not hung up about it." Of women who are alone most "want to have fun sex. This is a no-holds-barred period in their lives … they're more sexually adventurous and easygoing and while sex isn't the biggest deal in the world, they're more willing to take pleasure when it comes." Among the single women in the study, 10% have phone sex, 9% exchange erotic notes and e-mails, 7% go to strip clubs, 26% watch adult films, 14% use sex toys, dildos or vibrators and 26% masturbate. However, another report shows evidence that 89% of *all* women, single and married, practice masturbation, which is considered a "natural and harmless expression of sexuality."

Film producer, actor and comedian Woody Allen says,
"Don't knock masturbation, it's sex with someone you love."

In the interviews I conducted with widows and divorcées, I focused on how they handled their grief ... how they went about taking charge of their lives and how they attain *Fulfillment and Contentment.* I asked only *one* question about their sex lives: "Do you feel sex is important in your life?" A handful demurred but most declared sex *is* important. I was surprised when one widow, who had just dismissed the latest partner in her life, expressed her view: "Only women who have never experienced an orgasm would not be interested in sex." Then with a shrug, she offered that she herself masturbated and used a vibrator. "You are always sure you are practicing safe sex this way," she said, laughing.

Sex is good for your health!

There are several other medical studies, by British and American researchers that show there are physical benefits from the joy of sex. You may live longer, you use up to three hundred calories each time you have sex, your pelvic muscles along with your back, thighs, glutei and abs are strengthened ... and pain may be reduced. During orgasm the chemical oxytocin flows from the brain and appears to release endorphins ... the body's natural painkillers ... into your system.

The reports go on to offer recommendations to help single women attain better sex and enjoy its health benefits: avoid putting on weight, avoid smoking and overeating, exercise, and because your vagina becomes drier as you mature, you are encouraged to use lubricants and vibrators. Thus, even the medical profession suggests you ignore some of the old-fashioned taboos ... and *always* practice safe sex.

Expectations from your new partner

Once you accept your sexuality and have found a new lover, remember you are no longer the twenty-or-thirty-something swinger ... nor is he ... floating on that cloud of exhilarating love and youthful expectations. We women are not alone in our questions and concerns about our sexuality. One gynecologist I interviewed said that when women are young, they suffer menstruation and the pangs of childbirth. On the other hand, he went on, we men have our problems as we reach our middle and advancing years. These sex challenges that men grapple with (and which often can be treated with any number of medical techniques) are mercilessly flaunted in the media. The changes take their toll on men's emotions and their sexual performance: erectile dysfunction, softer erections, slower arousal and less intense orgasms.

However, according to the Harvard report on "Sexuality in Midlife and Beyond," some of the changes on the mind, emotions and body can open the door to a second or even a third chance for satisfaction that untested youth cannot offer. We realize the need for safe sex and have the experience, fewer inhibitions and a deeper understanding for our partners and for each other's needs and desires. These can be advantages that jump-start a different yet rewarding style of making love that dwells more on foreplay than trying to achieve orgasm.

Keep in mind: "Experience is golden!"

Conclusion

Though most of the information I include in this chapter is from reports prepared by experts, what I offer is merely an introduction to arouse your interest and suggest you pursue professional medical help if you require such attention. Call on your general practitioner or gynecologist, whom you trust, and who is aware of your medical and emotional history. If you have problems that you believe need more help, you might want to seek out a sex therapist. You'll find lists of places and experts you can consult for more advice in CHAPTERS 21 and 22.

CHAPTER 11

Financial Security

"Contentment is when your earning power equals your yearning power."

Anonymous

$\mathcal{F}$inancial security is a major factor in achieving success in your renewal process! This chapter is *not* about investment strategies. This chapter is about attaining and maintaining financial security for the time when you are *ready* to invest

No matter what your lifestyle has been, even if you have inherited a fortune, which is unlikely, your financial situation is and will be different from now on. Since you are experiencing a major change in how you live, reassessing your finances is a top priority. You have lost your partner. You are alone. Friends and relatives offer solace and consolation as you grieve, but the bottom line for managing your day-to-day living is in *your* hands.

Whether you were responsible for all the family finances, just handled the household expenses, left all to your significant other, or never gave money a thought, you now want to and have to take charge.

There was a time when most women were homemakers and depended on their spouses for financial support. Times have changed dramatically. Though women are a growing part of the workforce, we still must take time out to birth our children, nurture them and care for aging parents and other failing family members. Nonetheless, there are throngs of self-reliant twenty-first century women who face these challenges and are happy and thriving. You can join them. You, too, can have a well-paying job. You, too, can achieve financial security by taking advantage of the information, organizations, counselors and technology out there and get on the path to the independence you deserve. It may not be easy, but with a positive mindset and a dream, you can do it.

Jerry Lynch, President of JFL Total Wealth Management and a certified financial planner and adviser, recommends following steps offered in this chapter. They will take you through an ongoing process to achieve and maintain your financial security: start with a plan, establish realistic goals, make lists of *your* finances and analyze them, establish a budget, set a timetable and review your progress regularly. When you have built your nest egg, you can proceed to invest with guidance from a reliable financial adviser ... a certified financial planner.

Start with a Plan

Even if you had a plan before you lost your partner, your situation, which has altered substantially calls for a new set of rules. As you carry out the following steps and complete them, your template will develop. You will organize your income, expenses and savings along with your assets and liabilities in such a fashion that you will be able to fulfill your objectives. Your plan should be clear and flexible enough to handle discretionary expenses and changing goals.

Create an Emergency Fund

This is a cash account you start immediately. Though you will adjust the amount you set aside as you proceed with your plan, try to find enough cash now for ready access to cover unexpected expenses such as loss of your job, an appliance or utility replacement, an automobile breakdown repair, an uninsured medical expense or any other emergency. Once you have completed your plan/study, you should try to have enough available cash in the account to cover basic needs for at least six months. Should you need to dip into this fund, you will limit expenditures to those that are absolutely necessary. You should place the cash in a bank savings account, an interest bearing checking account or any other account where your funds will be available instantly or in a day or two.

There are ways you can raise cash to build your emergency fund by selling items you no longer need. Most families have two cars, but since you are now alone (and perhaps own two) you may sell the higher-maintenance vehicle. Have a garage sale. Or go through your home ... check your garden tools, television sets, electronic devices like computers, lap tops, cell phones, Blackberries, mobile devices ... select the duplicates or ones you don't use and place them on e-Bay or Craigslist. Not only will you be building your emergency cash reserve, you will be cleaning out your home of unwanted clutter that we all accumulate.

Establish Realistic Goals

Your first goal and continuing objective is to achieve financial independence ... being able to meet all your obligations, simply, to pay all your bills on time. Benjamin Franklin, our eighteenth-century diplomat, scientist, writer and philosopher said, "If you know how to spend less than you get, you have the Philosopher's Stone." (A substance that will turn base metal into gold.) For you, this may also mean being debt-free: paying off credit card charges and/or paying back money you owe.

The most important long-term goal is saving for retirement. If you have children, the next is setting up a fund for their college education. You may have other goals, such as replacing your kitchen or turning in your gas guzzler for a low-mileage hybrid, such as a Prius. The amounts you set aside for these goals depend on your net worth and your budget, which you will analyze as you prepare them.

Determine Your Net Worth

Make a list of your assets and liabilities to establish where your finances stand now. The difference between what you own (assets) less the amount you owe (liabilities) is your net worth. You may set up a schedule to include those here that relate to you, along with their value.

The charts on the following pages will assist you in this process.

Assets	Value
Cash	$ _____
Checking accounts	$ _____
Savings accounts	$ _____
Certificates of deposit	$ _____
Market value of home	$ _____
Market value of other real estate	$ _____
Vehicle – Blue Book value	
Autos	$ _____
Trucks	$ _____
Other	$ _____
Personal property	
Furniture	$ _____
Clothing	$ _____
Other	$ _____
Jewelry, art, antiques	$ _____
Life insurance (cash value)	$ _____
Retirement accounts	$ _____
IRAs	$ _____
Keoghs	$ _____
401(k), 403(b)	$ _____
Other	$ _____
Investments	
Stocks	$ _____
Mutual funds	$ _____
Bonds	
Corporate	$ _____
Municipal	$ _____
Other	$ _____
Other	$ _____
Total Assets	$ _____

Liabilities	Amount
Cash	$ _____
Mortgage	$ _____
Credit card balances	$ _____
Vehicle loans	$ _____
Home equity loans	$ _____
Student loans	$ _____
Other debts	$ _____
Total Liabilities	$ _____

Net Worth

Subtract your liabilities from your assets.

Total assets	$ _____
Less Total liabilities	$ _____
Net Worth	$ _____

Be as accurate and as honest as possible when you prepare your lists. Your assets should be more than your liabilities. Be cautious and avoid overvaluing your assets and undervaluing your liabilities. Your objective is to lower the value of your liabilities and increase your assets. These figures should be checked at least once a year to make sure you are achieving those goals.

Prepare a Budget

Repeating Benjamin Franklin, a budget is designed to help you spend less than you get! It is also much more. It shows you exactly where you are spending more than you should and is a tool that leads you to financial security. The lists recommended here are for tracking monthly figures. Since there are seasonal expenses, they have to be adjusted from month to month or can be included when you create a six-month or annual budget.

You may select the items listed here that apply to your situation and eliminate those that do not. The task, at first, can be challenging and time-consuming. However, if you persevere you will find it will take less time and be easier to complete each month. Also, you will be rewarded by meeting the goals you set for yourself..

INCOME

Item	Monthly Amount		
	Budgeted	**Actual**	**Less or More**
Salaries			
Full time	$ _____	$ _____	$ _____
Part time	$ _____	$ _____	$ _____
Bonuses, royalties, retainers, commissions	$ _____	$ _____	$ _____
Investment income			
Interest	$ _____	$ _____	$ _____
Dividend	$ _____	$ _____	$ _____
Other	$ _____	$ _____	$ _____
Income Totals	$ _____	$ _____	$ _____

FIXED EXPENSES

Item	Monthly Amount		
	Budgeted	**Actual**	**Less or More**
Mortgage/rent	$ _____	$ _____	$ _____
Vehicle loans	$ _____	$ _____	$ _____
Insurance			
Homeowners	$ _____	$ _____	$ _____
Vehicle	$ _____	$ _____	$ _____
Medical	$ _____	$ _____	$ _____
Life	$ _____	$ _____	$ _____
Taxes			
Real estate	$ _____	$ _____	$ _____
Income	$ _____	$ _____	$ _____
Loans			
College	$ _____	$ _____	$ _____
Home equity	$ _____	$ _____	$ _____
Other	$ _____	$ _____	$ _____
Retirement			
401(k)	$ _____	$ _____	$ _____
IRA	$ _____	$ _____	$ _____
College fund	$ _____	$ _____	$ _____
Emergency fund	$ _____	$ _____	$ _____
Investments	$ _____	$ _____	$ _____
Other	$ _____	$ _____	$ _____
Fixed Expense Totals	$ _____	$ _____	$ _____

VARIABLE EXPENSES

Item	Monthly Amount Budgeted	Actual	Less or More
Electricity	$ _____	$ _____	$ _____
Gas/oil	$ _____	$ _____	$ _____
Water	$ _____	$ _____	$ _____
Food/groceries	$ _____	$ _____	$ _____
Phones	$ _____	$ _____	$ _____
Vehicles			
Gasoline/oil	$ _____	$ _____	$ _____
Repairs	$ _____	$ _____	$ _____
Tolls	$ _____	$ _____	$ _____
Public Transportation	$ _____	$ _____	$ _____
Computer services	$ _____	$ _____	$ _____
Credit card debt	$ _____	$ _____	$ _____
Cable TV, DVDs	$ _____	$ _____	$ _____
Household	$ _____	$ _____	$ _____
Personal Care			
Hair/cosmetics/etc,	$ _____	$ _____	$ _____
Cleaning/laundry	$ _____	$ _____	$ _____
Other	$ _____	$ _____	$ _____
(Also, add 10% of total)	$ _____	$ _____	$ _____
Variable Expense Totals	$ _____	$ _____	$ _____

DISCRETIONARY EXPENSES

Monthly Amount

Item	Budgeted	Actual	Less or More
Restaurants	$ _____	$ _____	$ _____
Entertainment	$ _____	$ _____	$ _____
Vacations	$ _____	$ _____	$ _____
Pet Care	$ _____	$ _____	$ _____
Gifts	$ _____	$ _____	$ _____
Charitable contributions	$ _____	$ _____	$ _____
Fitness	$ _____	$ _____	$ _____
Other (Also, add 10% of total)	$ _____	$ _____	$ _____
Discretionary Expense Totals	$ _____	$ _____	$ _____

TOTAL OF ALL EXPENSES

	Budgeted	Actual	Less or More
Fixed	$ _____	$ _____	$ _____
Variable	$ _____	$ _____	$ _____
Discretionary	$ _____	$ _____	$ _____
Total Expenses	$ _____	$ _____	$ _____

INCOME VERSUS EXPENSES ANALYSIS

	Budgeted	Actual	Less or More
Total Income	$ _____	$ _____	$ _____
Total All Expenses	$ _____	$ _____	$ _____
Less Difference	$ _____	$ _____	$ _____

Again, your objective (according to everyone, not just Franklin!) is to make sure your expenses are less than your income. In addition, there should be enough leftover difference to add to a savings account that will become the basis of your investment portfolio.

Even though you have leftover income, it is imperative to analyze your expenses and discover items that can be eliminated or reduced. You will increase the amount in your savings account and attain *Financial Security*.

> *A quick and easy way to organize your financial progress ...*
> *if you use a computer... is to take advantage*
> *of a personal financial software program.*

Assessing Personal Financial Software

It has been said that most women find handling finances a daunting task. There are men who feel the same. When Ralph and I were married on a sunny June day several years ago, my mother suggested I leave the finances to my husband. I did. By the first of December, all we had was $50 between us. Fortunately, I am good with figures and money ... together we attained financial security for our family. *And that was before there were computers.*

Today, technological advances can simplify the organization of your finances. Among the many software programs, there are two that are most popular and are worth considering: Quicken and Microsoft Money. Both are reliable tools and are user-friendly.

It will take some time and patience to download and clean up your information from your bank. You may need permission to do so. But once that task is accomplished, and you have set up your categories, you can enter your transactions every day, or as necessary, and your budget is automatically updated. You make your entries only once and you will be able to pull up a number of different reports based on the input.

Another advantage when using a personal financial software program is help available in preparing income-tax reporting. Both Quicken and Microsoft Money flag items like medical expenses, donations, real estate taxes and others that may be used as tax deductions.

*Using your computer to manage your finances
is easier and faster than making your entries manually.*

Conclusion

This chapter offers information to help you understand the principles of financial planning and put you on your way to *Financial Security.* You may pursue any area in greater depth, on the Internet and in the myriad books available on the subject in book stores and libraries. Some of these are listed in CHAPTER 22 in the APPENDIX. Also, if you find the task as a whole too great a challenge, you can call on a certified financial planner ™ for professional guidance.

When you are ready to invest, Jerry Lynch, CFP, of Total Wealth Management suggests, "The key to investing is developing a strategy that you feel comfortable with at a risk level that is in line with your tolerance and then staying with it."

*"No one was ever meant
to remember or invent
what he did with every cent."*

Robert Frost, 1874-1963.
American poet

*If you live within your income
you'll live without worry
and without a lot of other things.*

Passage

Renewal to Adventure
(New Life Options)

*E*motional and physical renewal, along with financial stability, not only leads to *Solitary Contentment* and the exciting new adventures presented in *Part Two,* but empowers you and helps you take charge of your life.

However, though you have read *Part One* and carried out many, if not all, of the processes, you still may not have achieved the full renewal you hoped for. More than likely you have not. You are still grieving. You are still experiencing many, too many, of those painful emotions that you felt when you first lost your significant other. *Be assured ... you need not be concerned.* These feelings will ebb and flow like the tide. There will come a time when the sun will shine in your life the way it sparkles on the ocean's waves.

> *Nonetheless, if you find these emotions overwhelming*
> *you may still need to – and should – reach out*
> *to a grief counselor or*
> *others for professional guidance.*

Always remember, *you are not alone,* you never are. All of us who are bereaved suffer as you do. What you are feeling will go on and continue in varying depths for some time … for how long is different for each of us.

When the negatives return, try to pull up the good emotions for, from time to time, you *do* have them. Call on them. Dredge them up … the way you feel when you are with understanding friends … when you talk and laugh so much that tears trickle gently down your cheeks … and when you practice the suggestions in *Part One* that are so uplifting, repeat them. Often.

With the strength you, yourself, are building and with the help you receive from others you call on, you will gain the empowerment you are seeking.

Where are you in your search for renewal?

Do you feel the need to return and review *all* the chapters in *Part One* and carry out most of the suggestions again? *Or* should you select and reread the chapter(s) that help you the most and practice the exercises until you begin to feel empowered?

Or, are you ready to review the options in *Part Two* now, but want to delay carrying out any just yet? *Or,* are you not even close to renewal but you want to learn about the adventure options, *now?*

Or, have you achieved or almost achieved renewal and financial security ... and are ready to select and enjoy one or more options in *Part Two?*

Whatever your choice, it should be the one with which you are most comfortable. Also, whenever you decide to pursue an adventure, it is wise to include and repeat some of the helpful *Part One* tips in your agenda as well.

Before you undertake
your exciting new adventure(s),
make sure you are
emotionally, physically and financially prepared
to move on.

Part Two

New Life Options - Adventures

CHAPTER 12

Ready for Someone New?
A Significant Other?

"To say that you love one person all your life
is just like saying a candle
will continue burning as long as you live."

Leo Tolstoy, 1828-1910,
Russian author, "The Kreutzer Sonata"

*Y*ou may feel that there is no one else who can fill the void in your life after you have lost that loved one who has meant so much to you. **Leo Tolstoy** suggests that you are mistaken. He implies that the torch you carry for your love, that candle, will stop burning and there will come a time when you will welcome someone new. It may begin with sipping coffee with that someone at a café, enjoying an afternoon walk in the park, or spending an evening, a whole day, a week, a month together. The relationship may even stretch out through the rest of your years. And yes, you may love again.

There are those among my friends who agree with Tolstoy and gently tried to convince me that my candle would quench. Another romance? Never, not for me. I replied, *"Thank you, but I do not need nor want anyone!"* I would and could manage alone. There wasn't a man in the world who could replace my husband. Find someone like Ralph? Impossible! Nor would I want to. I continued to defy Tolstoy's premise.

Though I missed Ralph desperately and still do, I've never been lonely. I have achieved *Solitary Contentment.* I have more than enough to keep me occupied and distracted. I spend time at my desk on

117

finances and on my computer, I write, I garden, I read, I attend church, I travel, I phone my daughter almost every night, I relax on the couch with my pet next to me and watch a documentary on television and lots more, alone, contentedly. Yet after almost a year I responded to the gentle persistence of a man much younger than I and we began to enjoy pleasant times together. You may turn to CHAPTER 14 and learn how I changed my mind … not to adopt Tolstoy's view in its entirety but to open my mind and even my heart … a little … and share a part of my life with some one else.

> *What about the contention that women need men*
> *more than men need women … or is it the reverse …*
> *that men need women more than women need men?*

Do we *mature* women, indeed, need men in our lives, our intimate lives? Do *we need them more than they need us?* Or is it that we want men in our lives? Do women want them as companions, friends, lovers, providers, husbands, just to have them help with household chores … or all of the above?

In the 1928 tome, *The Technique of the Love Affair,* English author **Doris Langley Moore** opens her book with her narrator, Cypria, who considers herself an expert on things of the heart, saying, "Women are more guileful than men, but men have the advantage of being more necessary to us than we are to them." Later, she explains, "women need men morally, physically, socially and financially. Men's requirements of women are usually not so various."

Do You Agree or Do You Disagree? I … Disagree!

The distance of the place between the sexes in all phases of society has closed dramatically since the early years of the twentieth century. (Even so, we have much further to go.) Over the decades, women, at least most of us, have come into or have been made to come into our own. Why? The calamities of wars, the innovations of technology, better education and job opportunities, the acceptance of women in men's professions, legislation on behalf of women, the women's movement and the growing trend of single parenting by women, which forces us to become self-reliant and caregivers. To say nothing about the proven fact that women are survivors and most live longer than men and are forced to, and do, make do without them.

Katharine Meyer Graham spent her married life as wife, mother and homemaker until she lost her husband, Philip, the publisher of *The Washington Post* to suicide. Though she admittedly lacked confidence, she took on her husband's position and control of the Washington Post Company. Before long, she gained the respect of the newspaper staff, became a force in the publishing industry and was one of the twentieth century's most powerful and interesting women. Consider, on the other hand, how a man reacted to the loss of his wife: *Patricia Alden Austin Taylor Buckley,* a prominent fund-raiser and William F. Buckley Jr., the staunch conservative and founder/editor of *The National Review,* had been married for fifty-seven years. When Pat died, one of Buckley's friends said he "seemed dejected and rudderless." Bill's health declined rapidly and he, himself, succumbed within eleven months of his wife's death.

These are not exceptions, these are examples of the rule. I know and have interviewed women who also have survived and lived full, rewarding lives, alone or with a new companion. There are surveys and statistics to prove that women not only outlive men but we live long and well after we lose our significant others. (However, there *are* some exceptions even to this rule.)

What does this prove? That women may be able to thrive without men? Yes, but we have had love in our lives and we miss that love. Besides, it's comforting just having a man around the house ... or apartment.

Are You Ready for Someone New in Your Life?

Though you may be certain the time will never come when you will want or need a someone other in your life again, more than likely you will. When that happens you may feel as most women do ... some guilt and often a sense of desperation because you don't know where or how to begin. It has been months, years or even decades since you dated. Now that you are much older, the process of how to proceed appears overwhelming and the prospects of success seem hopeless. *Not to worry.* There are myriad offers of help to get you started, along with sweet-talking people who promise they will find you that "special someone." There are books, organizations, professional matchmakers, Internet sites and services all willing and eager to help ... and accept your contributions ... your dollars. *Just be cautious and beware.* I introduce you here to some of these techniques. For in-depth information and contacts, continue on to Step 2 of this chapter for lists of these bountiful aids to delectable matrimony.

There will come a time when you feel you are ready to consider and accept someone new after you have lost your loved one. It may be sooner than you expected, too soon ... you are lonely and needy ... a gallant comes along, takes advantage of your vulnerability, sweeps you off your feet and rushes you into a relationship or even marriage *before you are ready.* This can happen with disastrous results.

But no, you finally are in a firm position and will not be taken in. Let's say you are ready to begin your adventure to look and find someone because you:

are in control of your finances
are settled in a home where you are comfortable
have no stressful situations facing you
have set aside some time to look and pursue
want, not need someone
are prepared to be disappointed on occasion
hope to find someone quickly but you know you must be patient

There are other precautions to consider ... you may want to consult with your friends and members of your family, particularly your adult children. They are often reliable for recommending the *safest* possible dates. In fact, they are more than willing to tell you what you should and should not do and whom you should or should not date, develop a relationship with, or marry. I have had more than one person who say, "It's none of my business, but ...." Then they go on and give you advice.

Your situation is *not* any of their business! They have a narrow view of what you are facing. Yes, they are prejudiced in your favor and are overzealous about your well-being. However, they do not feel nor can they understand what you are experiencing. Hear what they have to say. Listen to their suggestions and objections. But *you* are the only one who knows. *You* are the only person who can and must make these critical decisions.

Shortly after she lost her husband, *Elsie* was influenced by her daughters to date and marry a widower they liked and who had been their father's longtime bowling partner. Elsie never bowled and never enjoyed the atmosphere of the alleys. She tried but failed to find common interests with her new husband. Within six months, she sought a divorce.

Tracy, a widow in her early 50s, was ready and finally felt secure enough to venture out on her own. Within three months after she began her quest, she attended a square dance with her son, Steve. She felt at ease and found it natural and rewarding to mingle with the crowd, though she had not been to a barn dance since college. Steve introduced her to John, a retired policeman who had been divorced for several years. He asked her to dance. He had been square dancing "since I was a kid," he told her.

They hit it off that first night and were partners every other Friday evening until the end of the season. She's happy living alone and seeing John now and then for a dinner date or a quiet evening at her home. They are getting close and somewhat serious. Would she marry him? He hasn't asked yet. And she hasn't decided what her answer will be if he does. If she says "yes," she wonders whether it will adversely affect their friendship. Steve avoids the situation but her daughter is skeptical. Tracy says she's old enough to make up her own mind.

So, You Have Met the Criteria for a Search and You Are Ready!

Are you sure? Do you have the time?

One of the major pitfalls of many new singles is having a long list of other priorities and failing to allocate enough time to the search. If your job, your children or grandchildren, your church, your hobbies, your dog or cat, your exercise program or any other person, pet or project takes precedence over or interferes with your search you may not be ready. Of course, these issues must be met but if they are pressing perhaps you should delay trying until you can devote the time to focus on finding that guy you want in your life.

A very busy widowed *Amelia,* who was running her deceased husband's auto dealership, spent an hour twice a week on the Internet trying to connect. Since she was attractive, intelligent and had an inviting online profile, she had scores of potential matches. However, by the time she responded to e-mail messages, many of the men were no longer available and she never managed a first date. Frustrated, she gave up.

Kelly, a real estate broker with two teenage daughters, was fortunate to have met someone who was right for her through a friend. Philip was a divorced college professor, had the summers free and asked her to take trips to the beach with him, attend outdoor concerts and sit together under the stars on his or her deck. "I have a real estate open house … an appointment with a client ... the girls want me to take them to …" she lamented. She accepted an occasional invitation and had fun, but Philip spent many sunny days and moonlit nights alone. When he returned to teach in the fall there was a new, unattached young woman instructor in his department who distracted him from Kelly. *Now Kelly continues to lament … for another reason.*

If you are ready, you will make the time.

Another caveat: Don't expect that new man you want in your life to seek you out. That won't happen! You cannot leave it to him or to chance. Staying at home, watching your favorite television program, reading a sexy novel, pining away and feeling sorry for yourself, waiting for the phone to ring or for your knight to ride up to your front door on his whinnying horse … will certainly only bring disappointment.

The ball is in your court ... you must make the effort to score a connection.

Start here.

The First Step:
Decide What You Want in a Lover/LTR

Since you are considering an LTR … *a Long Time Relationship …* (not someone for an occasional date), it's wise to take time to do some soul-searching as to what you can live with, can't stand and can't live without in a new significant other. As you contemplate, remember that no one is perfect (not even you) and, also, there is no one out there who is a mirror image of the loved one you lost … they do not exist.

Let's begin with the single status of your prospects: the widowed, the divorced, and the bachelor. Each has his drawbacks. The divorced man, particularly if he's been married more than once, is prone to break commitments. The never-married-single (since neither of you is in your teens or twenties and there are many n-m-s out there who are in their thirties, forties, fifties and older) is afraid to make *any* commitment. The widower is the best bet because if he has had a happy marriage he is lonely and believes he can be happy again with someone new. However, be cautious, he may be inclined to pine for his lost love.

The most reliable potential partner is someone who shares your basic objectives, situation, beliefs and principles. Among them are: religion, politics, family values, lifestyles, education and ethnic backgrounds.

There are always exceptions to the rules: Staunch members of opposing political camps working on the national level are *Mary Matalin,* the Republican, and *James Carville,* the Democrat. She serves as a GOP consultant, he is one of his party's strategists. They've been married for more than fifteen years, have two teenage daughters and from all appearances live happily together. They say they never discuss politics.

One of my close friends, *Kitty,* divorced and a Christian, fell in love with and married a handsome, widowed Muslim with a eighteen-year old autistic son, Jason. They have been happily together for three years. Kitty, who never had children of her own, takes pride in how much she has helped Jason. He has become more and more self-reliant and has developed social graces that belie his condition.

Along with assuring that you have some of the basics in common, determine how important personal traits are to you:

appearance	smoker or non-smoker
short or tall	body build
the silent type or a talker	professional or blue-collar
age	bald or a full head of hair
casual or somewhat formal	

And your interests:

movies	cuisine	television	travel
theater	keeping fit	hiking	water sports
dining out	cooking	reading	golf
dogs/cats	computers	texting	blogging

Learn about any baggage he may carry and determine if you are willing to share the load. There are men out there with chronic diseases or just over the hill looking for caregivers; others have addictions (gambling, drugs, alcohol), are in debt, owe child support or just want to shack up with a woman with an established, comfortable home.

Set your standards!
Don't deviate too far from them or at all.
And don't be misled by sweet talk and ardent, gallant gestures.

Step Two:
Where Do You Look for that New Man in Your life?

There are myriad venues where you can encounter single men as well as services that are available to help you connect with that "perfect match." You have to be willing to learn the current ways and methods of dating ... far different from when you were in your teens and twenties. Finding a new man can be like looking for a new home ... location, location, location.

The *safest* and most *reliable* places are gatherings of your relatives, friends and co-workers. Respond to and accept invitations whether the event is at the top of your list or not. You will be most comfortable and more at ease among those you know as you mingle among the crowd. Try to carry on conversations with the singles you meet but don't make quick judgments. You may reject that bald chap at first meeting, then learn he likes the theater as much as you. He may even ask you to the play you've wanted to see but were terrified to attend alone. And think twice before turning away from the one who is two inches shorter than you. He might cook Italian and French dishes the way you wish you could.

Some gatherings with friends you should not miss:

Cookouts	Graduations
Birthday parties	Dinner parties

| Communions | Weddings |
| Christenings | Bar and bas mitzvahs |

(I know a widow who met a divorced man at a bris. She's not Jewish. He is. They've dated several times and are getting serious.)

Special meetings at your church or synagogue
Class reunions and athletic events of your high school and college
Clubs and organizations to which you already belong

New places and new people:

Most local newspapers, magazines and websites have sections for singles looking for matches and carry lists of:

Nearby churches and synagogues

Supermarkets
(Visit early evenings after work hours and weekends.)

Sporting goods stores

Bookstores with cafés and reading areas
(Choose the spots with books on subjects that interest you.)

Hardware stores, like Home Depot and Lowe's
(on weekends)

Sporting events:
(with a woman friend who shares your interests)

Football, baseball, hockey, basketball, golf, horse shows, polo matches

Concerts, operas, theaters
(Discreetly look around during the intermissions.)

Festivals, craft shows

Art exhibits, museums, libraries, professional gardens, historical sites

Ballroom dance schools and square dances

Some of the more intimate place:

(attend with a close male or female friend)
Singles bars
Upscale bars at trendy restaurants

Starbucks or other coffeehouses
Outdoor cafés

Fishing on the Internet:

Once looked upon as a last resort, or even as an embarrassment, dating through Internet websites is often the first venue new and repeat singles turn to. Some consider it sport dating, having fun while looking, making a sport of *fishing,* not a serious venture.

There are several types of dating sites:

Ethnic dating	Senior dating
LGBT dating	Wealth and beauty dating
Christian dating	Specialty dating
Jewish dating	Canadian dating
Adult dating	

Some of the myriad dating websites:

BlackPeopleMeet.com	Mate1.com/Personals
CatholicPeopleMeet.com	MatureSinglesOnly.com
ChristianCafe.com	OnlineBootyCall.com
DateHookup.com	PerfectMatch.com
DatingforSeniors.com	PersonalQuest.com
Chemistry.com	PlentyofFish.com
DownToEarth.com	SeniorPeopleMeet.com
eHarmony.com	SingleParentMeet.com
JPeopleMeet.com	Singlesnet.com
LoveAndSeek.com	True.com
Match.com	Veggiedate.org

Speed dating

Speed dating is a fast growing phenomenon that has been around for some time but is now established as an exciting, rapidly-paced way to meet men/women. You spend five to eight minutes, depending on the event, with eight different prospects, selecting the one(s) you like for a second date. (With this method you don't waste time on a drawn-out first date when you come face-to-face and know he's wrong almost immediately.) Some organizers claim you have more than a 90 % chance of finding someone you will want to meet again and a 60%

126

chance he will want to see you for that second date!

How does it work?

It is sort of an adult version of musical chairs, with you, the woman seated at a table … and staying put. The men move from table to table. You carry on a conversation to learn as much as you can for the five to eight minutes … until the whistle blows and the men move to the next table. You make notes of the men you want to meet again and hand them to the organizers. The men do the same for the women. Usually, within twemty-four hours, you are e-mailed with your matches and are helped to make the connection(s). On occasion, the men are seated and the women move.

There's more. Anywhere from twenty to a hundred may attend an event, which usually is held in a local restaurant for a minimum fee. You may mingle among all the registrants, before and after the session and during intermissions, to meet others for your list. It's worth a try. You may make a friend or a business contact … or just have fun.

The high-priced promisers

There are several. I'll not name them since they are advertised on the Internet and in upscale publications. I was influenced by the "quality" of this type of matchmaker when I happened on a full-page ad in an airline magazine. I wasn't ready at the time but I did take the bait sometime later. I responded to a direct-mail piece from a company in the Washington, D.C. area that promised fifteen dates to begin with and more at a lower rate if none of first produced the "man of my dreams" or the "perfect match."

Of course, the flier did not include the cost. You were invited to meet with a counselor at the company's elegant, glass-walled suite in an upscale Maryland office complex. I'm embarrassed to tell you the high price I paid but I do so to prepare you if you are taken in as I was … over three thousand dollars for the program that my counselor, let's call her Nicole, recommended. There are others that cost much more. I managed to squeeze this *lowest-price offering* out of my budget. The men, of course, were charged the same and often bought higher-priced programs hoping to get the most attractive, sexy matches. All the men were guaranteed to be professionals and would more than equal my "requirements."

127

I filled out a multi-page questionnaire and suffered through a long interview about my interests, personal life and background. I was complimented, served tempting refreshments, photographed and jollied. I was shown a list of testimonials and clippings of glowing reports about the company in newspapers and on three major television channels. I was impressed with the thoroughness of the process. Even with my long career in sales I was taken in. I guess I was more needy than I thought since, at the time, I didn't see through the scam. I was assured that there were already several matches that were perfect for me. "I know of four offhand," said the beautiful, perfectly groomed, auburn-haired Nicole.

In retrospect, the procedure was akin to the misleading first step of the Madoff Ponzi Scheme, where you are made to feel unique, respected and qualified, with the right connections and the necessary finances, to be accepted into the fold of an exclusive club. I was eager and anxious to meet my first "match!" He turned out to be an amateur poker player who participated in competitions around the country ... I do not play cards. The second was a gun aficionado who arranged to meet me at a shooting range. I hate guns. The third had a belly so large I thought he was pregnant. I exercise and stay fit. The fourth was late for our date, did not apologize and monopolized the conversation. I am always on time and a good listener. He was a bore. I called Nicole ... not once but several times. She never returned my calls. Finally, the receptionist told me she was no longer with the firm. "Be patient," I was told by another counselor. I was, but I never heard from the company again. I gave up.

Perhaps I should have followed the example of two of the women I interviewed, who had similar experiences. Each rebelled after the first date. *Susan's* "match" was far beneath her educational level and his family background was vastly different from hers. *Mandy's* date was just a "jerk," she complains. They sued the matchmaker and both got back what they paid, over twenty-five hundred dollars. It took some doing but they won.

There are others who have been similarly deceived but do not try to recoup the exorbitant fees. They were (as I was at the time) too embarrassed to have their friends learn that they were looking for a lover and were duped in their effort. *Today* I would definitely sue!

Obviously, because of my experience, and those of others equally misled, I'm not recommending this avenue for finding the next man/ lover in your life. Nonetheless, I'm told there have been successful relationships and marriages made through these matchmakers. Try it if you are flush, can afford to lose your *investment* and can manage to live through a date with a jerk.

Step Three:
The First Date

You are ready. You have made contact with someone for that first date. Someone with whom you have carried on an e-mail correspondence and/or phone conversation, so he won't be a complete surprise … and who, so far, fits your criteria as a candidate for an LTR. You are a little anxious and perhaps expectant and hopeful … you are not alone.

Where do you begin? A place and time to meet: Agree on something public … a restaurant, a bistro or a café … where there may be others and perhaps friends you know. Preferably during the daytime for coffee, lunch or afternoon tea … old-fashioned but safe. Not too close to where you live, in case he's not right for you and you would not want to run into him at the supermarket or the bank sometime later.

What do you wear? Something attractive, of course, and casual … not too different from the way you look most of the time so when, and if, you meet again, you are the real you, the one you want him to get to know. Don't try to be someone you are not.

What image should you project? What do most men hope you are?

Independent, smart, energetic, confident … and a little needy!

Men admire women with the positive traits but they don't want them to be overwhelming. They, more than we, are enigmatic in what they truly want. They admire that self-reliant you, yet at the same time they fear someone who is strong and intimidating. They seek an independent woman, yet one who is wanting, with a need a man can fulfill … otherwise they feel useless and helpless. They must clearly know that they are needed, otherwise they will move on to someone else.

129

How do you fill that contradictory image? Be *feminine,* (as opposed to sexy unless sex is all you want) and somewhat *mysterious!* You can take control of the date … you, only you, not he, has what it takes … you are the woman, he is the man. *You* are the female in the encounter, so make the most of your gender. Before your date, think femininity. During your date, feel feminine … he's looking at your face, your eyes, your hair, your lips, your breasts. (Don't reveal your cleavage.) He's aware of your sex and sexuality … let him. You will naturally and subtly project your femininity and your self-image of confidence and intelligence. He just may want to see you again.

Mysterious? Let your date do the talking … (unless he's the silent type, then you'll have to find out what interests him … he won't be able to stop. That was my husband Ralph; he'd go on and on about science and technology.) *Your* man will be flattered and convinced that you like him. Tell him as little as possible so he'll keep coming back for more. "Keep him guessing." Think of **Scheherazade** whose life depended upon mystery. Each night she told the tyrannical sultan a fascinating story that ended on a cliff-hanger. He became so intrigued with the charade, he delayed her execution for "a thousand and one nights" and spared her … she was his last wife. You don't have to go as far as Scheherazade, but if your date appeals to you and you reveal your past life slowly and with mystery, he may end up as your LTR partner … or your husband.

You are on your own, now!
The rest is up to you.
Good luck!

Conclusion

Dating the second or third time around can be daunting. *Liz,* a widow, found her second husband on her first date out. Sadly, within five years he, too, died. She told me the year following his death was the worst she had lived. In an effort to lift her spirits, she started dating again. After several months, meeting with men she met online and finding none she wanted to see again, she was discouraged and stopped her search. Liz decided to focus on the graduation party she was planning for her daughter and her classmates. Tom, the widowed and very proper

130

high school principal, approached her after the graduation to thank her for how she handled "all those kids." She was surprised when he asked her to go to a concert in the local park on an evening she was free. They went the next weekend and to more throughout the summer

It can happen to you!

However, even if you are well-prepared after checking off the "are you ready?" list, taking all the necessary precautions and setting aside enough time for your search, there are delays and disappointments and, hopefully, some happy surprises. One of my female friends went to a speed-dating event and met two women more interesting than the men. They have joined our "Girls' Club."

Look upon your quest as an experience … experiment by trying the many ways of meeting new people. If you want to learn of alternative relationships, turn the page to the next chapter. This is the time in your life for adventure.

Enjoy your Solitary Contentment and begin or continue your search.

CHAPTER 13

Looking for a New Type of Relationship: a Woman Friend, Companion, or Lover, or a Male Confidant?

*"Love affairs between men and women do not last,
in contrast, great friendships among women
often endure indefinitely."*

Simone de Beauvoir, 1908-86,
French socialist, feminist, writer

*T*here is more than one type of relationship that will give you the rewarding life you wish for. There are several. As for that with a man ... despite **Simone de Beauvoir's** observation ... it can be rapturous and enduring. Perhaps the adoration alone may not last, but if both partners bring trust, respect and deference to the love affair, the union can go on for a lifetime. De Beauvoir, in retrospect, may have agreed. She and Jean-Paul Sartre, the existentialist philosopher, were longtime companions and sometime lovers until he died.

Try reaching out and testing the different kinds of bonding, particularly if you have been disappointed in your search for a new significant man. Or even if you have been successful, you may include another relationship that can be equally or even more rewarding than the one you had with your lost love. Having others in your life, men or women, contributes to achieving *Contentment.*

Women Friends

Here is where de Beauvoir shines. She believed in and encouraged friendships among women. No doubt you already have women friends

... and acquaintances. Start with the ones you know best and with whom you have already had positive interaction and sense may be willing to enter a closer relationship with you.

Make a list and be in touch with these first. Arrange to meet for coffee, lunch, dinner, a drive in the country, a walk ... a place and time where and when you will feel at ease just talking. Start by discussing the people and events you have in common. You may be surprised to learn that you share an experience that will bring you closer together.

I mentioned to **Daisy,** my real estate agent, that the reason I was looking for a townhouse was because I had decided to part from my live-in companion (see CHAPTER 14) and have a place of my own. She responded by saying that a year earlier, she had made up her mind to leave her then-significant other and was happier living alone. As we talked between checking out properties, we realized there were similarities to our "exes."

Sharing our emotions and sentiments was gratifying and helped us shed regrets and bitterness and accept the choices we made to separate. We found that this and other events that were taking place in our lives dovetailed. We came to realize that much about men and how we relate to them – and they to us – changes dramatically as we all mature. Daisy and I have become great friends and know we are not alone in what we are experiencing. We talk, a lot. And she found me an easy-to-maintain townhouse that is perfect for me and my new lifestyle.

When you perceive that a woman friend has a concern that is common to yours, pursue it gently until you know you can be candid and open yourself to her. More than likely, she will respond to your need because hers is similar to yours. We women are sensitive, caring, helpful and supportive ... that is our natural bent. Your friendship should flourish as you come to rely on each other more and more ... whether it is having a long, involved discussion over coffee or dinner, or a short, reassuring phone conversation.

If you have exhausted all possibilities in your quest to find that unique woman friend or have moved to new community, there is always the Internet. You might try girlfriendsocial.com which is free. Girlfriend Social "connects women with new female friendships" and is for women only who are looking for platonic female friendships. "You can sign up to attend fun, female-only girlfriend events in a safe and friendly environment." Among other woman-friendly websites are newfriends4U.com and SocialJane.com.

A Woman's Group

I was fortunate to be welcomed into "The Girls' Club" (an informal group of local women) when my hairdresser learned that my "younger man" relationship had ended. There are about ten of us, *most* are professionals, independent and financially secure. All of us were single ... divorced or widowed ... when we joined. It is an informal club that came about and continues without any structure. We meet for dinner or an event, in twos, threes or more as the spirit moves us, or at the spur of the moment.

One or another of us is usually available for a favor or special need: meeting a parent at the airport, babysitting a child/grandchild or even help with online dating. We encourage or discourage each other on how to handle our relationships with men. We respect the family situation of each member and readily give advice and support. We listen, but of course we make our own decisions, good or bad. Two members have married, three have LTRs, others are dating or still looking. Our group may be unique but if you can form one in your community you will share good times and have help from many fine women.

Move-In Woman Companions and/or Helpmates

There are women who find themselves alone and seek a quasi-business relationship with another woman. They are not looking for a friend, though friendships often develop as time passes. These women are companions, housekeepers or helpmates wishing for a pleasant home. They move in and share household expenses or exchange chores for rent or are paid an agreed-upon rate. Occasionally, they are thought of as boarders using a guest room and private bath, but in truth they are, or can become, much more.

Maxine, a neighbor of mine who lost her husband when she was in her early forties, happened on an ideal situation. *Marie,* a young French woman who had been a nanny for Maxine's sister's family while the children were small, moved in with Maxine temporarily until she was ready to return to France. The women filled each other's needs so well that Marie stayed on and is still with Maxine after twenty-five years. They also have become devoted to one another. Early on, Maxine converted the unused storage area over her garage into a pied-à-terre for Marie, so each has privacy when she wishes some space.

If you choose to consider such a situation, you can check the want ads in your local paper or place an ad of your own with your requirements. There also are domestics agencies that will help you connect with a woman who is right for you. Typically, the most reliable resources are your friends, your place of worship or members of organizations to which you belong.

A Warm Relationship with a Woman

Women don't hesitate to openly show affection to one another emotionally and physically. When we meet, we hug, we embrace, we kiss, we laugh, we cry as we exchange greetings and talk about intimate things. We are spontaneous. This often spills over into greater closeness as our lives change. Relationships between women that begin as friendships, at times, go beyond the casual to others that are closer and express deeper feelings, feelings of love, particularly after the loss of the man in their lives.

When we find ourselves alone, our need and desire for understanding, sympathy and sensitivity have few limits. *Sally* and *Wilma,* both widows, were spending an overnighter together. Dressed in their gowns and robes, they discussed the good times of married life as they sat in front of a warming fireplace. As they began to doze off, they slipped into bed together and fell asleep in each other's arms. "I was reminded later," Sally told me, "that the experience with Wilma gave me the same comfort I would share with my daughter ... then five years old ... when she'd climb into bed with me seeking reassurance."

There is an innocence and a human fulfillment in such closeness and it can happen in other ways. I had a phone call from *Bette,* a longtime friend and also a widow, the day after a summer party we spent at the home of Fred, a widower acquaintance of hers. His live-in significant other was out of state on a business trip. I had left early. Bette was

136

spending the night since she would take a plane home the following day. "Too bad you had to leave," she said, "the rest of us had a cooling swim in the pool. Then, everyone else took off. I was exhausted and was in the guest room bed in no time. I heard a knock on the door and Fred came in. He crawled in beside me. *No! Nothing happened!* He just lay there holding me for a while and left. It was an intimacy we both seemed to need."

When you experience a similar incident of intimacy
make sure it is sincere and relish it!

An Alternative Relationship

In our society, a marriage between two people of the opposite sex … a man and a woman … has long been considered the only respected, accepted union and the one entitled to create a family with children. For the most part, these "values" still hold true. However, throughout history, other twosomes have been treated with scorn, ostracism and criminalization. Today, in many parts of our country, there are communities that accept them, encourage them, ignore them and/or welcome them. The armed forces have eliminated the "don't ask, don't tell" stipulation that was designed to protect them. They, of course, are the homosexuals, individuals who are sexually attracted to others of the same gender … gays and lesbians.

Among widows and divorcées in their thirties, forties, fifties and more who now are alone, there are some who, for the first time, find themselves attracted to other women. In the twenty-first century, most lesbians "come out" early, in their teens and twenties. The older women have grown up in an era when homosexuality was not included in our lexicon … same-sex love affairs were out of the question and the couples ostracized. Back then, women married, had children, stayed wed until "death or *divorce* do us part."

With the changing times, the feminist movement and greater sexual freedom, many older women are reassessing their sexual orientation. Some had manifestations of lesbianism much earlier, but ignored them or were afraid or ashamed to acknowledge them. Now, inspired and liberated by the openness of respected professional, celebrity and political lesbians, they have come out or are in secret lesbian relationships. Among the well-known are actresses *Ellen DeGeneres, Lily Tomlin, Meredith Baxter, Drew Barrymore* (a bisexual), *Tammy Baldwin,* the first openly gay United States congresswoman, and *Mary Cheney,* the daughter of former Vice President Dick Cheney.

Lesbianism has flourished throughout the centuries and dates back to the 6th century BC and the island of Lesbos, the root of the word and the home of Greek poet *Sappho.* She wrote about the lives of women, their rituals and relationships, concentrating on feminine beauty and her own love for young women.

In the nineteenth century sexologists began to categorize this sexual orientation as a medical problem, a congenital disease, and in some cases a form of insanity. Brilliant women accepted the challenge and the lesbian subculture was launched. There were several lesbian salons in Paris, attended by noted women like *Colette, Gertrude Stein* and *Radclyffe Hall*, the author of *The Well of Loneliness*. At one time, Berlin had as many as fifty homosexual clubs and cafés. In America, Nobel Peace Prize Winner *Jane Addams,* socialite *Mabel Dodge* and renown poetess *Edna St. Vincent Millay* were among several acknowledged lesbians of the time. Greenwich Village and Harlem were the hot spots with saloons the popular attraction, particularly for tourists. Though interest in such gathering places continued through the early twentieth century and cooled, the culture continues and grows.

More and more women are acknowledging this sexuality and find happiness and satisfaction in a lesbian relationship. If you are wondering if you are a lesbian or bisexual, there is a plethora of literature, information and professional guidance available to help you decide and move on. Though there is evidence that as women grow older they are often more sexually attracted to other women, *Lisa Diamond,* a University of Utah researcher, says, "A safer conclusion to draw is that as time goes on, women have more opportunities to discover that capacity. They have more diverse relationships. Their life patterns change. Their careers change. They become more expansive in their thinking, more open-minded."

You can explore this way of life by checking your library and/or the Internet, where there are numerous websites on the subject such as lesbianlife.about.com and sageusa.org/about/. Enjoy the adventure!

A Confidant of the Other Gender

If you are not ready for a lover and/or have a bevy of women friends but crave masculine company, consider a *Confidant of the Other Gender,* a close, platonic male friendship. There are men out there who have a need for and would welcome female companionship but, as you, do not want to enter a committed relationship. They are the singles who are among the recently (or even longtime) divorced or widowed, the confirmed bachelors and gay men. Though they often hesitate to reach out to women, they are open to being informally approached at family or neighborhood affairs. It may all be up to you. Once you have made a connection, you will find you have a companion and a sympathetic confidant. If there are none in your circles, try asking your understanding women friends, those whose husbands belong to men's organizations or work in companies with a predominance of male employees.

Jo Ann, the most gregarious member of our Girls' Club, had three such confidants before she married. The "guys," one, a confirmed bachelor and two gays, continue to be her good friends. Together with one and sometimes two, she would attend cultural events and family and other gatherings. She shared experiences with them, called on them for advice, had discussions over a glass of wine at the local pub or entertained them all at a cookout on a summer evening around her pool. They were and still are her pals.

Conclusion

Interaction with one or more human beings of either or both sexes contributes to a fulfilling life. Love with a man is only one way of achieving your ultimate goal of a rewarding, satisfying relationship. Explore these alternatives. The journey can be as exciting and sometimes more so, than reaching your destination. Once you have launched your trip, stay open to all the possibilities. You may be surprised to learn that in a new, unexpected partnership you have more control of your identity and you will be able to enhance your *Solitary Contentment* during the times you choose to be, or find yourself, alone.

CHAPTER 14

Consider a Younger Significant Other

"What is so dreadful about a sensible, older woman
piloting the life of a younger man?"

Plutarch, c. 42-120 AD,
Greek biographer, philosopher

$\mathcal{M}$ost of us marry young, in our twenties, to our significant other, who is about the same age. Years later, when our partner has long been gone and we begin to think of dating again, we find there are few unattached prospects in our age group.

You are alone.

Expanding your circle of friends to include a potential companion is a worthwhile venture and may contribute toward building your *Contentment.* If you are approached by a younger or much younger man, don't reject the advance handily just because it is unconventional. You would not be the first woman to enjoy the company of a younger man. However, learning about his background and intentions is paramount!

By happenstance I experienced such an encounter. Within a short time after I met young Ken, Sandy, a mutual friend of ours, took him aside. "Take care," she said, "Victoria is much older than you."

Ken smiled, amused, as he told me. I was puzzled.

What was there in a possible friendship between us that he should be cautioned about?

My husband Ralph had been gone a very short time. Another man in my life was as foreign to me as taking a spaceship to Mars. The thought of someone else close to me – other than my husband who had been three months older than I – was out of the question! A younger man? Never!

It was later, much later, that I realized what Sandy was inferring – it was when I learned about disparate-age relationships. She knew about them then. Why should it matter to her? Ken and I were both adults

Ralph and I were always avid play-goers wherever we lived and continued our passion when we moved to Virginia three years before he died. We attended performances and supported the local community theater here. It was on a beautiful sunny Sunday morning, early in June, that I had visited Ralph in the nursing home as I did every day. Later, I went to the "friends of the theater" annual meeting in a nearby country inn.

Since Ralph and I had always gone together, I felt very much alone in the reception area among the noisy, genial crowd of actors and members of the group. I wandered off to the expansive, glass-walled porch, where the only person in the room was a pleasant-looking man in a yellow sports shirt and khaki trousers. He was sampling the hors d'oeuvres. I approached him, introduced myself and told him I lived on the mountain outside of Haymarket.

"I'm Ken ... Ken Tyler," he replied. "I work *in* Haymarket!" We talked about the theater. He told me he was vice president of a woodworking company and through his job he contributed sets for the performances. When the luncheon meeting began, instead of joining others, he sat next to me. During pauses in the program, we discussed our interests. Of course, we are both theater buffs. I told him that Ralph always attended plays with me but he was very ill.

Among Ken's vitae were that he was fifty-one, divorced, lived alone and had a serious, long-distance relationship with a California woman his own age. I learned more about Ken at that first meeting than I knew about many of my longtime friends. To my surprise, as we parted, he offered to accompany me to the opera whenever I needed an escort. "Anytime," he added with a chuckle, "I *do* have a tux."

Four days later, Ralph died. Though the doctors predicted he would leave me soon, I was devastated. Late one afternoon the following week, Ken appeared at my front door. His stay was brief. Afterwards when he'd come to visit, he'd linger longer. Slowly, we became friends

... we went out to dinner, attended the theater, other arts events and opera, *sans tux.* On occasion, we would spend an evening at my home with my friends, mostly women.

Several of these friends, in private, expressed concern for me. They tried to dissuade me from a relationship with Ken. They said that since I lost my husband and I was alone, I was vulnerable ... *vulnerable to the whims of a younger man?* I had heard of disparate-age relationships but, at that time, I knew little about them. I acknowledged the warnings and went about researching why I might be cautious as my friends suggested.

I learned that these "unions" are relatively common. Older women often have younger male friends, companions, confidants or even lovers, and some marry them. On a regular basis, tabloids and television report cross-age romances ... of older men and young women, as well as aging women and younger men ... about celebrities, wealthy CEOs, movie stars, athletes ... and ordinary people. Among many seasoned actresses who have chosen to take younger men as husbands are **Mary Tyler Moore, Olivia Newton-John** and **Joan Collins. Dinah Shore** and a nineteen-year-younger Burt Reynolds were an item in the 70s.

Hollywood has not neglected the theme. **Gloria Swanson** and William Holden starred in *Sunset Boulevard* about an aging actress and a young writer. The much-panned film, *Moment by Moment,* links **Lily Tomlin,** as a forty-year-old divorcée with John Travolta, a nineteen-year-old parking lot attendant. Then there is *White Palace,* starring **Susan Sarandon** (who in real life had a younger significant other) as a forty-three-year-old burger-joint waitress and her twenty-seven-year-old advertising executive lover.

This is not a contemporary phenomenon ...
it has its roots in ancient history!

Older Women/Younger Men Relationships Over the Centuries

Though these relationships have their origins in early history, by no means have they been accepted out of hand. In fact, there are moral and religious objections to such couplings with edicts advocating that women should be younger than their husbands to secure the patriarchal system.

The male drive to dominate the family structure is decreasing and has not precluded cross-age coupling. Older women and younger men continue to have strong sexual, emotional and intellectual attractions to one another. There are written records of proof that throughout the ages these unions existed, flourished and were gratifying to both the woman and the man. Further, such relationships resonate today and have varying degrees of social acceptance.

Here are just a few of many from recorded history

There are countless Greek and Roman myths about involvements of goddesses with young gods as well as with young mortals. Some goddesses conferred eternal youth on their mortals by making them gods. Though most of these relationships were for love and to fulfill sexual desires, some carried out their divine authority. Goddesses were worshiped and, as women, were the dominant gender throughout the ancient Western universe. They would choose to couple with younger men to control their destinies and "pilot their lives."

It was in the Arab world, during the sixth century AD, that Muhammed, at twenty-five, married the forty-year-old wealthy widow *Khadija*. With her fortune and his sword, he founded the Muslim religion.

In *The Canterbury Tales,* Geoffrey Chaucer tells of *Alison, the Wife of Bath,* who outlived five husbands ... the last two were several years younger than she. She was traveling to London to seek out a sixth, also a youth.

When she was sixty, English *Queen Elizabeth I* had her thirty-year-old lover, the Earl of Essex, beheaded for refusing to carry out her commands in Ireland, a crime and betrayal. Heartbroken, she never recovered, died two years later, still mourning her loss.

In the twentieth century, French author *Colette* penned the novels, *Chéri* and *The Last of Chéri,* based on her relationships with much younger men. It was always she who ended the affairs.

If you are interested in more, you can browse the Internet or check the history section of your local library and you will discover countless others, and in great detail.

144

So why the caution from my friends?

They warn that a younger man will take advantage of you ... he's interested in sharing ... sharing your finances, your possessions, your home, your lifestyle. He is charming, attentive and may even declare his love for you to accomplish his objectives. He may, but he just may be sincere.

Ken *was* sincere.

I heard what my friends had to say and decided to continue our developing friendship ... with caution. We attended performances of the arts, we visited museums and festivals, enjoyed the beach and wandered parks. Once a week, we'd have dinner at my home and talk. Ken encouraged me tell him about Ralph, our fifty-eight-year marriage, our careers. He filled the pauses of silence by talking about the jobs he had that took him to places around the country and overseas ... and his experiences as a volunteer fireman. His kindness and understanding were helping me through my grieving.

It was an evening in September, a little more than three months after we met. Following dinner at my home, we sat in my favorite room which had large windows looking out over the countryside. I sat at one end of the sofa, Ken at the other. We relaxed. He opened the conversation by saying, "I've written a poem for you." As he drew a slip of paper from his shirt pocket, he continued, "Would you like me to read it?" How could I refuse? "It's called, *Victoria's Heart.*" And so he read – it was a tribute to my love for and the loss of my husband.

I was moved. Ken understood how alone I was. Strangely, though he had a romantic involvement, it was long-distance, and he, too, was alone. We had similar interests and were enjoying each other's company. He respected me and I him.

After some time, I sensed that Ken might be interested in a closer relationship. I was not. I could only see him as an understanding, compassionate friend. Not only was he much younger – and I had yet to learn about older woman-young man relationships – but there was his same-age girlfriend, Jennie.

I decided it was time to look for someone I might consider as a companion someone older. This search ... far from pleasurable, satisfying or productive ... is recorded in CHAPTER 12: *Ready for Someone New? A significant Other?* If you have not yet read this chapter, you may find it revealing and helpful. Though I was not successful, there are women who *do* find what they seek.

After several months dating older men I gave up. I relented and returned to seeing Ken. I was torn. It was not fair to him or to his friend, Jennie. He would visit her in California and she would come East. Even when she was here, he would spend an hour or two with me. I tried to end the relationship but Ken persisted.

In February, two-and-a-half years after we'd met, Ken was booked to go to California. The day before he was to take off, he called. "I'm not going. Never again! I've told Jennie it's over. May I see you tonight?" It was Valentine's Day! I said, "Yes." Was this the commitment I wanted?

I'd always insisted he make a choice and be with Jennie. For several weeks, I felt uncomfortable and remorseful. Finally, I concluded that it was Ken who had made the decision, not I. In May, we vacationed in France. On our return, Ken moved in with me and we began a rewarding, contented life together.

Soon there were challenges in Ken's life ... it was he who was in need of support and understanding. Ken had seen me through the most difficult time in my life. Now I was there to help and provide for him as he battled and won a bout with a serious illness. This and other problems Ken was facing transformed me into the caregiver in our relationship.

What others think

Friends and family frown upon and more often object to the older woman/younger man relationship. Mine have warned me often and many have been surprised to see that it can work, while others refuse to accept that it can. They have a right to be concerned. You *are* vulnerable. **Virginia**, a retired fashion designer, widowed, sixty and elegant, had an on-and-off-again relationship with her forty-eight-year-old younger man. She called it off abruptly and with finality when she learned she was supporting his gambling addiction.

Yet, don't hesitate! It is *your* life and *you* make your decisions. They warn that the younger man will take advantage of you. Yes, he may, particularly if he offers to handle your finances and help you change your will to include him. Be cautious. Does he work? Where does he work? Who are his friends? However, if he needs an advance from time to time, don't deny him out of hand ... just keep the reins short. The joy, the care and the love he gives you may be worth your consideration. *You* must take care! Weigh the pros and cons before you take the plunge.

The give and take in the older woman/younger man relationship

Age-disparate relationships are often sparked by a common interest, as was theater for Ken and me, which set the stage for genial conversation during our first meeting. There is a subtle physical aspect that is more significant to the attraction. The older woman, though vulnerable because of her loss, has a certain grace and confidence through what she has achieved in her career and/or through her social interaction. The young man may be drawn to her because she's on a higher level than he is in the same field ... the arts, design, decorating, films, writing, philanthropy, the law. Even her vulnerability may attract him. For her, his appeal is his youth, his handsome physical features ... his face, his athletic body, his full head of hair ... and no, he's *not* an old man ... he's *young*. And, he's attentive and listens to what she has to say. Above all else, they both are lonely.

Some of the gives and takes

Statistics show that women live longer than men. Let's start with that. Losing *one* husband/lover who was the same or close to your age is more than enough. It is likely that your *younger man* will outlive you and ... who wants to experience another such loss? However, I know a widow whose younger man died, and soon thereafter her second was killed in an accident. Chaucer's Wife of Bath was widowed by the death of two younger men, her fourth and fifth husbands. But the odds are against this happening to you.

Obviously, you have lived longer than he. He respects you. He benefits from your experience, stability, knowledge, financial situation and wisdom (maybe not all, but some of these). You can introduce him to people, places and adventures he could not hope to find on his own.

Your younger man, generally, will be a gentleman. He will open doors (literally) for you and will be your escort to events that you might avoid if you were alone. All these, along with helping with chores and just being there as a friend to talk about things that interest you both. Some are great cooks. Since these men *are* younger they can keep you current with the latest trends in language, music, films and technological advances. Consider, too, that your younger man, once you have gotten to know him, will make you feel safe and secure in your home.

What about sex in your cross-age relationship? It's up to you. You don't have to deny the desire. Young men take *pleasure* in *pleasing* their beloveds and in return *you* experience *pleasure* and a renewal of the woman you once were and hope to be again.

We, as women, are caregivers who nurture and nourish those we love. Your younger man benefits from your need to give. For you, there are occasions – as time passes and you mature (a euphemism for growing older or aging) – he'll be there to take care of you. Your younger man does not have to be a husband, lover or live-in companion. He may be a confidant, a good friend or a casual acquaintance. Or he may be someone who is happy to escort you to the theater or a special occasion when you feel more comfortable accompanied by someone of the opposite sex. He often takes pride in being seen with you. Having such a relationship with a younger man, when you choose, can put you in charge of your life and permit you the privacy and the perfect *Contentment* that you seek.

If a younger man crosses your path, don't discount him.
*He may turn out to be **your** younger man!*

FAST FORWARD: This chapter was among the first I wrote when, many, many months ago, I began compiling information, researching, interviewing and writing this book. Since then, Ken and I have gone our separate ways. You may wonder why, since I write glowingly about him and encourage you not to discount a younger man. I still suggest having an open mind to men who are younger than you.

In my case, after eight years, it was time. I sensed it coming three years before it happened. For Ken, it wasn't another older, younger …

or any woman. Perhaps it was that we no longer had the need to fill the supportive roles we wanted when we first met. I look upon those years with Ken as a transition from the loss of my husband, to living alone now … and loving it. I may be alone but I'm never lonely. I can call, count on and share great thing with scores of friends, mostly women. I enjoy a busier and happier life. I have *Solitary Contentment*.

In today's world,
an eight-year relationship is longer than many!
And, there just may be
another younger man in my life!

CHAPTER 15

Unconditional Love, a Pet

"Animals are agreeable friends. They ask no questions,
they pass no criticisms."

George Eliot (Mary Ann Evans),
1819-1880, English author

*D*o you have a pet? If you do, you're already on your way to *Contentment.*

The emptiness you experience from the loss of your loved one is being (or can be) filled with the unconditional love of a pet. If you don't have the traditional dog or cat or are allergic to them, there are other lovable creatures that make great companions and will always requite your love. For any emotional need you have that you wish granted, you will find a special critter out there that wants to be there for you. It can be love at first sight when you spot the one you didn't even know you were seeking.

You may read this chapter straight through to learn what's out there.
Or, if you know the category you may want, just flip through the pages
to that breed or species and find details (sizes, personalities, traits,
etc.), which will help you decide on the pet that's right for you.

Are you ready to adopt your unconditional love and live happily ever after? *If you are, don't neglect a feathered friend or even the rare or exotic,* particularly if you have reason to avoid a cat or dog. Bringing a pet into your life, especially when you find yourself alone, can be surprisingly gratifying and comforting. It's worth venturing out for the unusual or the unexpected. Take the plunge and try, because you'll never know unless you do. Or add that "out-of-the-ordinary" to what

151

you already have and create a small menagerie.

Veterinarian **_Deborah Cronin, VMD,_** co-owner of the Califon Animal Hospital in New Jersey, encourages developing the animal-human bond and validates the importance of having friends, both human and animal, in our lives.

I had two adorable, loving, cuddly puppies … I always refer to them as puppies since even as they matured, they were still small enough to sit on my lap together. Misti (Mistral de Provence), an elegant whippet, along with Otto (Otto Edouard Leopold von Bismark, I'll have you know,) a month younger than Misti, a deliberate, low-slung dachshund, grew up as a team. I was grateful for their presence. particularly when they seemed to sense my loss and the absence of their master when my husband died. A more affectionate, well-mannered pair never traversed this planet and each has carved an indelible mark on my heart. Misti lived to the ripe age of sixteen … a year-and-a-half later Otto followed his love to puppy heaven. I'm sure they're happy snooping out new friends and tumbling about on fluffy white clouds as I mourn them.

I continue to miss Otto and Misti so much that I do not have the heart to replace them. Instead, I decided to adopt a pet far different from my puppies. After months of deliberating, I selected a feathered friend … a four-week-old, beautifully marked yellow cockatiel. She/he (a cockatiel's sex is not determined until it is eight or nine months old) was the most handsome of the lot I chose from. It has taken a while, but finally just before I learned whether my pet were Chéri or Chérie we began to bond. For weeks, I wondered if it would ever happen. It has been worth the wait. My cockatiel is a girl … Chérie sits on my shoulder, crawls around my back and my chest, pulling herself up and down with her beak, squawks loudly in my ear, pecks my neck and my chin and, from time to time, casually drops a speck of poo on my shirt. She rubs a soft wing against my cheek to assure me she belongs and will be devoted as long as we both shall live. I may still adopt a puppy or two for I'm sure Chérie would enjoy perching on their backs. Envision the picture! Imagine the joy!

What is your wish?

Will you look for something small and cuddly, large and furry, long and smooth, tall and slender, tiny and crawly ... or something that sings, croaks, screeches, barks, whimpers or purrs ... or something that runs, flies, glides, gallops, lurks, lopes, slithers, climbs, lunges, burrows ... or something that snuggles, hugs, nestles?

What will you consider besides a cat or dog?

I list many of the following with tongue in cheek and I do not recommend them out of hand. However, it is interesting to realize that there are avid collectors who have a strong attraction to their exotic pets. Here are a few:

- Llamas, horses, tigers, lions, elephants, cows, camels, calves, mules, donkeys, goats, lambs, sheep
- Groundhogs, raccoons, sloths
- Mice, rats, squirrels, rabbits, guinea pigs, pigs, hogs
- Fish, goldfish, snakes, frogs, lizards, alligators, crocodiles
- Insects: spiders, butterflies, moths, bees, wasps
- Feathered friends: parakeets, parrots, cockatiels, cockatoos, macaws, canaries, crows, ostriches, chickens, ducks, geese, hawks, owls, swans, guinea hens
- Other: urchins, monkeys, gorillas, gerbils and many more.

(Just keep in mind that it is illegal to own some of these species.)

*On the following pages, I cover in some detail
several of the species, including a few of the unique and exotic
that are most commonly accepted as pets.*

Cats and Dogs

*"It often happens that one is more humanely related
to a cat or a dog than to any human being."*

Henry David Thoreau, 1817-1863,
naturalist, poet, essayist

Kittens – Cats

Sally, a lawyer who lost her husband to a heart attack when he was in his mid forties, had her hands full handling both their clients after he died, because they were partners in the law firm they founded together. They had no children but their days were full ... they were a loving couple, inseparable after meeting at law school. They traveled together, had an active social life and were volunteers in their church. Sally grieved for Robert, but she knew she had to continue to keep involved and she did. She missed him ... dreadfully. The short times she spent at home in the evenings were painfully lonely. But she wasn't ready nor did she want to take the time to meet someone else. One evening after dinner at the home of a client, Sally's host took her to a corner of the family room, where she showed her a mother cat proudly purring over a litter of five kittens. It was love at first sight. Sally adopted two of the furry bundles. Not only are they comforting companions when she comes home after a long day, but on special occasions ... to the surprise and delight of her clients ... the kittens hold court on the couch in her office reception area.

Sally's kittens fill a void in her life. But there are many reasons why they, both as kittens and then cats, make wonderful, adorable pets. The American Humane Society offers some that are compelling and may convince you to adopt one or more:

- Cats need only fifteen minutes a day to satisfy their need to play.
- They are very clean and bathe themselves.
- Cats can be left alone while you work.
- Cats may reduce your blood pressure and fight depression and loneliness.
- A cat's purr is calming, soothing and relaxing.
- Cats do not need much space and are comfortable in small areas like apartments and recreational vehicles.
- It is easy to litter-train a cat.
- Unlike dogs, you do not need to walk a cat.
- Cats *do* have nine lives and will give you twenty years of companionship.
- Animal columnist **Joan Lowell Smith** adds her own reason for adopting a kitten which perhaps is the most meaningful of all. "Cats are cute and cuddly." Just what you want on a winter's night when you come home from work and are all alone.

154

Sally fell in love with a pair of mixed-breed cats, but there are more than eighty breeds from which to choose to please you but any one you select will quickly find its way into your heart. Here are just a few:

The Mix ... is the most popular feline ... ninety percent of cats are mixed and therefore come in different sizes, shapes, colors and personalities. Each will adapt well to its new home, depending on the care and attention you are prepared to give.

The American Curl ... is distinguished by the unusual curl of its ears. They curl back from its face toward the center of the back of its head and look more like cowlicks than ears. The kittens are born with straight ears that start to curl within ten days. Their coats are soft and silky and require little care. They are playful, friendly and love to curl up on the the laps of their owners.

The Burmese ... has many characteristics of a dog. They like to follow their owners around and are easily trained to fetch. Their coats are short and satin-like and come in warm shades of champagne, sable, blue and platinum. As kittens they are lively and somewhat clumsy as they try to jump beyond their range. They have large, soulful eyes and as they mature they grow charmingly irresistible and often run the household.

The Maine Coon ... is a long-haired feline that adapts well to harsh winters like those in Maine, where it was first recognized as a breed. A sturdy, medium-to large-size cat, it is known for its intelligence and affectionate personality. The Maine Coon is a great companion, takes quickly to children and animals, particularly dogs, and is a top-notch mouser.

The Munchkin ... remains kittenish in personality and medium in size all its life. Its legs (by natural mutation) are short but it scampers about even more quickly than its long- legged cousins. Its bushy fur requires care but its playfulness and affectionate nature are happy return rewards. It is not a loner, prefers a companion and enjoys the company of adults, children and other animals. It's a hoarder and will seek out your jewelry and knick-knacks and hide them in its bed and out-of-the-way places.

The Persian ... is, obviously, named after its country of origin.

Its beauty, its long flowing coat and gentle personality make it the most popular *pure feline breed*. The Persian seeks a serene, secure environment but will be reassured and adapt quickly when you give it love and attention.

The Rag Doll ... is a large, fluffy long-hair who goes limp in your arms, its bed or wherever and whenever it is so inclined ... just as its name implies. Rag dolls are fearless with sturdy bodies, can weigh up to twenty pounds and may play rough on occasion. But they are loyal and loving and respond readily to your care.

The Sphynx ... is a very special, exotic and social breed. Their unusual bodies appear hairless, but they have a fine down that is like soft suede. The Sphynx are inquisitive, full of energy and mischief, and are show-offs, wanting to be the center of attention.

You are certain to be captivated by the first or second kitten you encounter, but learning about the cousins of the one you select ... only some of which I mention above ... can be worthwhile and intriguing. There are the Abyssinian, the American shorthair, the Bengal, the Norwegian Forest cat, the Ocicat, the Oriental Shorthair, the Russian Blue, the Scottish Fold, the Siberian Forest cat, the Singapura, the Somali and dozens more. You may turn to CHAPTER 21 on where to find more information about them.

Puppies – Dogs

> *"Wanted: A dog that neither barks nor bites,*
> *eats broken glass and shits diamonds."*

Johann Wolfgang von Goethe,
1749-1832, German philosopher,
poet, dramatist

Though it would make you wealthy, I doubt this is a dog you want to encounter on a walk in the park or choose to own, even if you could find one. However, if Goethe were alive today, I'm sure he would still be running his ad in search of this unique investment.

Among all the pets in the world, puppies and dogs are the most desired and sought after. Filling the void of your lost love may be the most meaningful reason for you to have one as your companion. However, psychologist, social scientist and author **David Niven** sets

forth in his book *100 Simple Secrets Why Dogs Make Us Happy,* ninety-nine more reasons why you should adopt an adorable canine. Among his most provocative "secrets" are that they:
- don't hesitate to show their affection
- will help you live a longer, more meaningful life
- are not judgmental; they don't question your decisions or choices
- are consistent in their behavior; they don't have good and bad days as we humans do; only on occasion are they ill and if they are, they appreciate your care
- are the source of undiminishing, unending joy
- are always happy to greet you and wag their tails in excitement
- make your house feel like a home
- help you think positively about yourself and the world around you
- help you exercise since they like to take long walks with you
- play for fun, have fun and make you have fun, too
- provide a connection in your life and make you feel less alone
- will sense when you have a solemn mood and help you recover

Most importantly, you can develop a unique relationship with your puppy and with the dog it grows into and a bond that is everlasting. There are more than a hundred-and-fifty breeds with different shapes, sizes, colors, dispositions and personalities ... but each is the companion who is always there for you and gives you *unconditional love.*

The breeds fall into six categories: sporting-gun dogs, hounds, herdings, terriers, toy and companion dogs and working-Artic-guard dogs. Though *toys* and *companions* are considered the choice house pets, don't overlook those in the other categories.

Experts differ on which are the top ten most popular puppies/dogs among canine owners. I've reviewed several lists and have made my own of ten, not in order of popularity but because all make great companion dogs. I offer them with some of their most desirable characteristics and leave it up to you to decide which will give you unconditional love. (The names of other popular breeds follow.)

The first two appear on most lists.

The Labrador Retriever and the Golden Retriever ... share many traits that make them the top favorites on most lists. They are intelligent, patient, gentle, playful, affectionate and, of course, great retrievers. They are medium in size, both standing just under two feet tall. A labrador comes in different colors, and obviously the golden is golden. The labrador's jaw is square, the golden has a gently shaped, long nose. Both are handsome.

The Dachshund ... with its long body and short legs is a badger dog that chases small animals and digs in gardens and under fences. They are playful, courageous, intelligent and lively. Since doxies are strong-willed, it takes patience and care to train them. But they reward you with loyalty and a great deal of love. Besides, they are great watch dogs.

The Papillon ... is one of the most elegant, vivacious and dignified of the toy long-haired breeds, weighing about four to eleven pounds. Its name is French for butterfly because its ears flare out like butterfly wings. The papillon is playful, full of antics and a show-off. Yet it is gentle, patient and affectionate to the point of being possessive and jealous. It is one of the most intelligent dogs, easy to train and alert to unusual sounds, making it a dependable watch dog.

The Poodle: the Toy, the Miniature and the Standard .... Contrary to the attribution of "dumb blonde" to this canine breed, poodles are exceptionally intelligent. They are alert, active, obedient and easy to train. Each size is similar in disposition and carries itself with an air of dignity. Their curly hair, always a solid color, needs constant care and clipping. The standard is over fifteen inches tall and weighs forty to fifty pounds; the miniature is ten to fifteen inches and fourteen to sixteen pounds; the toy is up to ten inches and weighs six pounds.

The Yorkshire Terrier ... is a rugged little dog with the admirable, lovable traits of large dogs. Their ability to learn varies from obstinate to bright, but with perseverance any Yorkie can be trained. They are possessive of their owners as well as their toys and food. A Yorkie prefers adults, will bark shrilly at strangers but its voice can be curbed if taught when it is still a puppy.

The Cavalier King Charles Spaniel ... is timid as a puppy but soon becomes a spirited, graceful toy breed when you give it attention and care. It is cheerful, playful, gentle and even-tempered, has an affinity for adults and loves to snuggle on your lap and in your bed. Yet they enjoy the outdoors and chasing squirrels, birds and chipmunks.

The Beagle ... a small-to medium-sized breed, handsome in color and configuration, is renowned as Snoopy in the comic strip *Peanuts*. Beagles are even-tempered, gentle, amiable and almost "merry." Though they are single-minded, determined and often difficult to train, they are obedient, lovable and small enough to cuddle. With their great sense of smell and inclination to bark, beagles make superb watch dogs.

The Shih Tzu ... is the ideal apartment dog and the perfect companion for you if you must live alone. They are the most charming, sturdy and robust among the toy breeds. The Shih Tzu is outgoing, intelligent, affectionate and devoted to its owner. It makes a delightful traveling companion and is friendly with other animals and adults.

The Boxer ... is a large, intelligent, dignified dog, standing twenty-one-and-a-half inches tall and weighing from fifty-two to seventy pounds. His coat is short and smooth in colors of fawn, brindle or white with striking shades of red. The boxer, easy to train and quick to learn, is agile, full of energy and needs lots of active play. He is protective, will worship you and, if necessary, he will defend you. Since he is very curious and highly spirited, he must be kept on a close leash to keep him out of trouble.

These are only a few of the popular breeds among the companion dogs from which you may select. Others include the bulldog, the Irish setter, the German shepherd, the collie, the Bichon Frise, the whippet, the Pomeranian, the Chihuahua ... and many more. Pedigreed puppies and dogs tend to be expensive and may not fit your budget. However, you may save a great deal on the initial cost of your pet by securing a rescue dog for a minimum fee by contacting your local rescue shelter or checking the search engines including PetFinder.com. You will be rewarded with a pet that will adore you and in turn you will have the satisfaction of *rescuing* an animal from a dismal fate by giving it a *forever* home.

Once you have chosen that very special pet there are preparations you must make and items to purchase before you bring home your "unconditional love." If it is a puppy, you will need a crate and house-training pads ... for obvious reasons. You will need a water and food dish, plus, of course, the food itself, chew toys of rawhide or plastic and a leash. For any canine you should set aside a cozy corner with a comfortable cushion or quilt where it knows it can sleep, nap or just escape to its own space. And be ready for the veterinarian's bills, spaying or neutering, worming (if not already performed by the kennel or rescue shelter) and regular check-ups ... and be prepared as well as for the unexpected. My whippet needed joint replacements, first for one hind leg and then a year later for the other, each cost $1,500. But she repaid me more than in full with unconditional love.

Ponies and Horses

Though you cannot hold ponies or horses on your lap and hug them, they are warm, friendly and some *are* considered pets ... especially the pony. If you choose to adopt one ... or more ... you will be rewarded with a happy welcome, a nicker (a soft sound) as he/she hears you approach the stall. Then it will snuggle against your shoulder with its nose, seeking that carrot treat you always bring. Horses and ponies require more care and attention than smaller pets, but they are a joy to ride or just to watch as they trot and gallop in an open field. They can play a special and important role in your life and fill the hurtful void after you have lost your loved one. These animals support your need for exercise with a physical, fun pursuit. They can provide you with an all-encompassing involvement that helps you put aside your feelings of loss and loneliness for long periods of time.

Ponies

Ponies, of course, are the smaller of the equines and most often are pets for children. However, they can also be your step toward owning a horse or fill that nagging emptiness in your life.

Betty and her husband Spencer, an officer in the local bank, never had children. They were exceptionally close, spent hours together at their lovely home, entertaining, visiting friends, traveling, and attending theater, opera and concerts. But after Spencer died, when they were both in their early fifties, Betty was desperately alone. She had never held a job nor had she been involved in any activities on her own. Though she continued to entertain, her home, quietly empty after her guests departed, brought her bittersweet memories of how she and Spencer would sit by the fire and relive the fun-filled evening. Nevertheless, she counted her blessings because she was left with a comfortable income, her mortgage-free home on a large piece of fenced land and a small barn.

One late afternoon while visiting neighbors, Jody and Roger Harris, her host took her for a walk on the property and introduced her to a Shetland pony grazing in a grassy corral. The creature looked forlorn, as lonely as Betty herself often felt. The pony had been the pet of the Harris' twin girls who were at college and no longer could care for the animal. "It's difficult for us," Roger said, "since as you know we are both at work during the day." By the time they returned to the Harris home, a deal had been struck. Within a few days, Silver, the pony, had a new home in Betty's barn ... spanking clean and filled with straw, feed and hay.

But that was only the beginning. Betty went on and adopted another, then another pony until each of her six stalls was filled. She rises early each morning, and, alone, takes care of her ponies ... mucking out the stalls, grooming the animals, feeding them and turning them out to pasture. She lingers long enough to let them know she loves them and visits them throughout the day. On special occasions she invites the neighborhood children for pony rides. Now the ponies are Betty's family. I've heard her say, "They're better than children, always there for you. They are loving and affectionate and don't grow up and move away." Betty no longer has time to be lonely.

If you decide to adopt a pony, you'll find scores of breeds to select from. A few of the most popular are:

The Connemara ... takes its name from the region on Ireland's West coast. Connemaras are strong, hardy, great to ride and can also be good jumpers. Most are gray, but others may be black, brown, roan or chestnut.

The Fjord ... the Vikings' fighting "horse" has unique, striking markings. Dun in color, its mane stands upright and its legs have

161

zebra stripes. Also hardy, the Fjord is a great ride and an all-around pony.

The Icelandic ... though small in configuration, also is often called a horse. Icelandics are unusual because they do not move as other ponies; instead they pace a smooth trot and tölt ... a running walk, which is very fast, yet a comfortable ride.

The Shetland ... is the smallest of the British breed and originates on the Island of Shetland, north of Scotland. They are small, tough, popular, intelligent and challenging. They come in several colors: gray, brown, black, dun and chestnut.

The Welsh Pony Section C ... is one of four types of Welsh ponies. It is a Cob, which indicates it is chunky and can support a child or an adult rider. Only solid-color equines, the Cobs are handsome, have a great deal of stamina and can be worked all day.

A pony can be your pet and more ...
it will give you that escape of a physical, fun pursuit.

Horses

"When you are buying a horse, take care not to fall in love with him,
for when this passion hath once seized you
you are no longer in a condition to judge his imperfections."

Sleur de Sollesell, 17th century author

If you decide to adopt a horse, riding is most likely your reason. Should you be fortunate enough to have your own barn, your horse will get to know you, acknowledge he's yours and will greet and treat you as his human. He'll snuggle his soft nose against your shoulder, seek out the carrots you always bring and noisily chomp away. A horse you ride at a private farm or public park on a regular basis will get to recognize you and also become your friend.

There are several breeds of horses ... thoroughbreds, quarter horses, Morgans, Arabians, Westerns are just a few. The way to begin if you are a novice is to take lessons at a nearby barn, then decide which type of riding you prefer ... pleasure riding on wooded trails, jumping, barrel racing, dressage or showing in any of the categories.

162

Whichever you select, you will find there is something unique about riding a horse ... an anonymous horse lover tells it best: *"Riding is a partnership. The horse lends you his strength, speed and grace, which are greater than yours. For your part, you give him your guidance, intelligence, understanding, which are greater than his. Together you can achieve a richness that alone neither of you can."*

Though your relationship with a horse will fill a special role in your life, you will not be enjoying quiet or playful evenings at home with your creature. You will spend hour upon hour dressing properly, tacking up and preparing for your lesson or waiting for your turn in a show. Then there are costs you incur that go far beyond that for a cat or a dog ... lessons, appropriate clothing, equipment and riding gear. If you decide to own your horse, you will have to pay for its food, its stall, shoeing and veterinary fees. However, within the horse community you will find people who happily spend more on their animal than on themselves. My daughter is one of them and she owns three horses.

However, if you choose a horse and to ride, you will be rewarded with hours of incomparable pleasure with an irresistible and dedicated companion.

A Feathered Friend

Linda, a divorcée, found she needed company in her shop even though she has a successful decorating business with two part-time assistants and several regular clients. She adopted two red-and-green macaws who squawk and talk to her in their floor-to-ceiling cage, as she cuts fabrics, stitches draperies and upholsters furniture in her workroom. If her birds become a distraction when she confers with customers in her conference area, she closes the door, but takes comfort knowing the birds will be there when everyone has left. Each morning when she opens her shop door and is greeted with clamor, any sense of loneliness she feels vanishes.

There are many reasons why birds make good pets, particularly if you never had one before. They bond with their owners and are near the top in intelligence of "animal" pets. They learn quickly. They are inquisitive, adapt readily to new surroundings and perform delightful, human-like antics. They are easy to care for, require little or no grooming and need little space because they can stay in a cage. Social creatures, they are easy to train and are less costly than most other pets. Long-lived, most will be with you for fifteen to twenty years and some as long as seventy-five to a hundred. Best of all, they are colorful and pretty to look at.

Despite their myriad advantages, there are several caveats to consider when you begin to shop around for that handsome winged creature. The larger the bird, the more expensive it is to purchase ... (some cost up to $5,000 ... others as little as $25) ... to house, to feed and to care for. The large birds can make great, genial companions, but they are noisier, messier and more demanding of your time and attention. Their behaviors vary ... from wanting to be touched to ignoring you when they choose to remain in their cage. It's worth researching the different species to learn which will best adapt to your lifestyle.

Here are some of the birds that are adopted most often:

Parakeets or budgies ... or more exactly, *budgerigars* ... are perfect if you have never adopted a bird. They are small, hardy and come in an array of glorious colors. They take less care and require smaller space than larger birds. Most whistle and sing and there are those who speak a word or two. They live twelve to fourteen years.

Cockatiels ... are medium in size, the most beautiful of bird species, and are available in several combinations of brilliant colors. Members of the parrot family, they like to whistle, sing and mimic noises they hear like radio music and the ring of a phone. Some can be taught to say a few words but they prefer to squawk. Their life expectancy is fifteen to twenty years.

Finches and canaries ... are pretty and little, only five inches in length. Because of their size and inclination to bond with their own species, they require little attention and make great pets to watch. They live up to ten years.

Lovebirds ... only six inches long, are the smallest of the parrot species. They have the intelligence and personality of a macaw but are quiet, making them ideal as pets if you live in an apartment or town house. Lovebirds' life span is about twenty years.

African greys ...After researching hundreds of breeds and species for this chapter, I've decided that when I'm ready to add to my small menagerie, I'll adopt an African grey ... if my cockatiel Cherie allows me. Primarily gray with white faces and legs and red tails, they are the most intelligent among the parrot types, have an amazing ability to reason, are incredible mimics and some can develop vocabularies of over two thousand words. Long lived ... to seventy-five and older, greys often outlive their owners.

When you choose a feathered friend, you will learn that you have adopted an affectionate pet that will bond closely with you. It will remind you regularly with a squawk, squeak, whistle or song that you belong together forever. But make sure you research the species to select the bird that will best suit you and your lifestyle.

The Unusual, the Rare and the Exotic

You will join the ranks of the famous when you venture beyond the accepted household pet and seek out the unusual, the rare and the exotic. I'll not go beyond the borders of our country to places like India where maharajahs have elephants, tigers, reptiles or panthers in their backyards. I'll confine my famous to our presidents. Most were drawn to the typical household variety of cats, dogs or birds, like *Franklin Delano Roosevelt* and Fala, his Scottish terrier, and *Dwight D. Eisenhower* and Heidi, his Weimaraner. There are others who for whatever reason ... for photo ops, to exhibit their sense of adventure or just for the love of animals ... found the unique intriguing.

Our rugged, robust twenty-sixth president, *Theodore Roosevelt,* was the most outlandish of our nation's leaders in his fondness for pets. Among the more than twenty in his menagerie were a pig, a badger, a piebald rat, a garter snake named Emily Spinach, several Guinea pigs and a one-legged rooster. *Calvin Coolidge* was not far behind with more than sixteen exotics ... two raccoons, a donkey, a goose, a bobcat, two lion cubs, an antelope and Billy, a pygmy hippopotamus. *Harry Truman* owned a boa constrictor; *Herbert Hoover,* Weejie, a Norwegian elkhound and two alligators; *James Buchanan,* an eagle; *Martin Van Buren,* two tiger cubs; *John Quincy Adams,* an alligator and silkworms, and *Thomas Jefferson,* two bear cubs. *Andrew Johnson* adopted two white mice he found in his bedroom and fed them every day. There are many more, but these are the most bizarre.

If you are daring, have the means, the time, can handle the unexpected and can put up with waiting for approval and the licenses you need to adopt the unusual ... go for it. However, again, though they will surely divert you from your loneliness, I suggest you find a cute little puppy or a sweet, furry kitten.

Make sure you spend enough time to research
each breed or species that interests you
so you find that special creature who is perfect for you.
Whatever you choose you'll be able to count on your pet for
Unconditional Love!

You'll never be alone again!

CHAPTER 16

Your Dream Job

"Work is the only thing. Life may bring disappointments,
but work is consolation."

Marcel Proust, 1871-1922,
French writer

"Work isn't to make money; you work to justify life."

Marc Chagall, 1887-1985,
Russian born, French artist

*D*espite the view of celebrated author Marcel Proust, work is *not* the "only thing" in one's life. There is much, much more that comes first. There's love, family, faith and whatever else you hold dear. On the other hand, work, as he maintains, *is* consolation, an escape from grief, despair, loneliness and disappointment. Yet, if work does become the "only thing," it can control your life and harm and destroy you and all you treasure.

Chagall's tenet is closer to the mark ... that we work to justify life. But we *do* need to work to make money to *sustain* our lives. Then, we may choose to go on to fulfill our destinies and express the creativity that drives us. In this way, we hope to make a contribution and give back.

You have been grieving. You've been out of touch with or neglected some aspects of your life; now you are back on track and ready to move on ... with your work. But you have some doubts. Though Proust's and Chagall's tenets strike a chord, you're not sure exactly how they relate to you. Do you have a job? Is it your dream job? If it is, you may stop reading this chapter and go on to another. Do you want to turn your current job into your dream job? Do you want to reinvent yourself and find a new job that is the one you've dreamed about all your life? Or are you not employed and now want a career to *sustain yourself* and/or to *justify your life*. Whichever path you choose can be a rewarding journey.

When **Shelly** was twenty-nine, she lost her husband and had two little girls, nine and six, whom she had to support and care for, alone. She had been a stay-at-home mom and had never worked full time. She felt fortunate to find an entry-level job repairing electric typewriters for clients of IBM. As she rose up the ranks to manager, she said, "the work was neither well-paying, prestigious nor gratifying. But I paid the bills and helped one of my daughters get her BA in history. The other chose to work after a stint in a community college." Sixteen years later, Shelly opted to try the developing field of technology. Her daughters were married, independent and with families of their own. This time, Shelly, a creative, quick learner, soon was making a six figure salary and was able, at last, to buy a home of her own.

Nonetheless, she felt unfulfilled. She was fifty-five. If ever she were to be happy in her work, she realized, she had to consider other options. Looking back, she remembered that even as a teenager, she had enjoyed photography, taking pictures of flowers, trees, landscapes, gardens, gazebos and other charming buildings. Her interest in nature never waned. She designed and thrived on planting around her newly purchased home, often working until dusk forced her to go indoors. She began to spend time in the library, on the Internet and visiting nurseries and arboretums. She was on the road to her calling … *landscape design!* She quit her job, invested in a year-long course at a university- affiliated institute of landscape design, where she earned her masters degree. She went to work for a landscape firm for two years, then set herself up in her own company. She exhausted her savings. It took three years until she had her first year in the black. In response to a question about advice for others, "You have to take risks," Shelly said, "and persevere. The hard work is worth it. I have my dream job." She has much more. She has the joy of seeing the color and beauty she has given the world and the green she's added to the environment.

Turning Your Current Job into Your Dream Job

You are happy in your field and may have another reason or two to stay but still you are not content. You don't want to leave but you are uncomfortable with the climate in the workplace, the assignments you have been given, how you are treated (given credit for your work), how you are ranked among your co-workers ... or all the above. It may be that you have been unable to focus on your job because of your loss and your attempts to adjust to your new life situation.

Where and how do you begin? Pinpoint your most important objections and frustrations and be honest with yourself by deciding what *you* can do to overcome them. Ask your manager/boss/superior for a private discussion. No doubt he/she has been aware of what you have been experiencing and will offer support. Once you have established a mutual understanding, many of your objections may fall away. However, it is wise after your meeting to maintain a subtle, open line of communication with your superior. **Mark Schnurman,** a career coach, suggests several tips that can help you improve the way he/she views you and will help turn your work into that *dream* job.

The most important consideration, Schnurman notes, is understanding and adjusting to your boss' style of communicating: group meetings, face-to-face, one-on-one, phone, e-mail. If you prefer yours over his, try to adapt to his. If you cannot, you may be better off making a job change. If you manage to get over this hump, go on to Schnurman's tips which will make your boss more aware of you and your contributions toward the company's goals.

First: Develop a good, ongoing relationship with him/her. Make a point of speaking briefly and in a friendly manner with him every day, not always about work issues but about his hobbies, pets or other interests. However, don't make it *too* personal. Try a casual comment if you run into each other in the parking lot, at the water fountain, as you pass in the hallway ... or if you happen to be in an elevator together. Making the most of these encounters will relieve any awkwardness and clear the air.

Second: Volunteer for different projects. Offer new suggestions and solutions to current ones that will move your department forward.

Third: Compliment him on how he has handled a meeting or prepared a report. He is human and likes to be appreciated, as much as you. Thank him for any positive comment he makes about your work and for his expertise and guidance. It doesn't hurt to apple polish a little from time to time (or "brown nose," according to Schnurman). "But, be sincere," he says, "just don't go overboard."

Fourth: Own up to a mistake if you have made one. Apologize calmly and sincerely in private and show how you have corrected the error.

Fifth: Above all, keep your manager informed about your work and your progress. If he doesn't know, he can't credit you for your contributions.

Focusing on all the aspects of your current job will not only help you transform it into your dream job but will help relieve much of your grief. If you have difficulty improving your work situation on your own and still want to stay in the same field and company, you may choose to invest in a career coach who will help you through the process step by step.

Reinventing Yourself and Finding Your Dream Job

You've made the decision to look for a new job and have *no doubts* about making this change in your career. You are not alone. In today's world, men and women are making two and sometimes three moves to other fields during their work lives. We are fortunate that there is legislation that protects job seekers against biases. Yet there are caveats to remember ... you may find a few employers who still discriminate, though subtly, when it comes to age, sex, race and physical appearance. But don't let that stand in the way of your search.

Your *first step* is to choose a field you prefer. Be introspective. Make lists to learn your likes, strong likes, dislikes, strong dislikes and hates as they relate to work. Analyze, understand, acknowledge and accept them.

Review the following lists of questions/conditions and write down your responses. Be as specific as you can. Your answers should help you define the type of work you want and are best suited for, as well as indicate the type of organizations and places where you may wish to apply for your next job:

These questions are to jar your mind and memory.
You may learn what you seek before you answer them all.

Do you prefer to work ...
 alone or in a team?
 indoors or outdoors?
 at home or in an office?
 in one place?
 or traveling

What are your ...
 talents?
 skills?
 values?
 interests?
 hobbies?

Which fields interest you ...
 the arts?
 sciences?
 travel?
 education?
 medicine?
 health care?
 fashion?
 technology?
 publishing?
 other?

Do you want to work in
 Government?
 a small company?
 private industry?
 a large corporation?

Where do you choose to work?
 near your current home?
 a select city in your state?
 a select state?
 out of the country?

anyplace?

Other:

Are you a *people* or *"thing"* person?

What are your *best* qualities, talents and skills?

What do *others* tell you that you do best? What you hear may reveal your calling.

What type of position do you want in your chosen field?

Is *salary* a major consideration? Or will you settle for less in order to work in your dream field, dedicate yourself and ultimately earn what you deserve?

Once you have analyzed your replies and made your choice you should be ready to proceed.

The *second step* is learning what your selected field requires in background, capabilities, talents, skills and experience. You are determined to make the change and you will do the necessary research to learn what they are and transfer those you already have. If you are lacking any or all, there are ways you can acquire the expertise you need and prepare yourself for your new field.

Several years ago, when I lived in Virginia and served on the board of the College of Visual and Performing Arts at George Mason University, I had the occasion to talk with the director/president of the largest Virginia opera company. I asked him the path he had followed to achieve his prestigious position. "I worked in management in private industry," he explained, "but I was always interested in music and all the arts. I enlisted as a volunteer in the opera company. I enjoyed it, was good at it and I accepted a low-paying, entry-level job. Over several years, I worked my way up." It was obvious that he loved what he was doing.

Volunteer work is only one way to learn about a *new field*. You can work toward a degree as Shelly did in landscape design. You can enroll in a community college and take regular or adult study courses. Or you can attend a school dedicated to a special field, such as medicine, health care, cosmetology, culinary arts, technology, photography, cinematography, journalism, communications, the military, real estate, law, accounting and the fine arts: theater, music, painting, sculpture and more. You can go online or study and research your subject at your own pace.

Internships and part-time jobs are other avenues that you can pursue to get the hands-on training you need. Seek out a professional in your field and ask to interview him/her. She should be willing, helpful and flattered that you asked. Not only will you gain solid information but it may lead to that internship or part-time job, the ground-floor experience you are seeking. Don't hesitate to ask if you find an opening during your meeting. There may even be a full-time job for you after you have put in time as an intern.

The *third step* is projecting the image you should have for your new job. How should you be perceived by your prospective employer? What level of professionalism does your new position require? Though the work you will be doing may call for clothes that are casual, sporty or a uniform, always wear proper business attire for your interview. Avoid revealing and sexy outfits. Your posture, grooming and make-up, as well as your language, including e-mails, phone messages and letters, are all reflections of who you are. Be on time for appointments, not too early or late, and do not speak ill of former employers or co-workers. Be positive and upbeat. Develop your image deliberately ... do not leave it to chance. If you are not already there, you will find that you will become what you set out to be.

The *fourth step* is preparing your résumé. I offer, here, a few guidelines, but for in-depth help you may choose to turn to books and websites on the subject such as rockportinstitute.com.

There is no rule that requires you to produce a standard one, two, or three-page résumé. Your document should reflect your image and personality and not be a dry list of your past positions. A résumé is the vehicle designed to open the door for an interview and lead to a job offer. Employers often receive hundreds of résumés, which presents you with a challenge to have yours stand out among all the rest. You are selling yourself, you are writing a professional document ... an advertisement about *you!* If yours is not run of the mill, if yours is unique, you might get what you seek ... that interview.

Your presentation may include a cover letter and a four-part résumé: an introduction, an assertion of your abilities, qualities and achievements, proffered honestly and powerfully, a back-up listing of your education and former positions with descriptions and a summary.

Your letter should address your interest in and knowledge of the company to which you are applying and why you are a proper fit. Here is where you may mention that a *respected* employee recommended his company to you, if that is the case. If you are moving into a new field, explain why you are making the change and how you will be able to transfer your talents and past experiences to your new position. You may indicate that you bring an open mind and a fresh approach to the industry. If you are reentering the job market or are in mid-career, here is where you may explain why. The tone of the letter should be professional, yet cordial and sincere.

Adapting your résumé for each company to which you apply will help gain the favor of any interviewer. The first line of your introduction, like the headline in an ad or commercial with an unexpected but applicable twist is where you will catch his/her eye. You have studied your field … you can create a "stopper" that will draw him in to read more. But leave something out to make him want to know more about you. A little innocent mystery doesn't hurt. Employers often skim parts two and three to make sure you are qualified, then move on to the summary, where you summarize, of course. Be sure to add some personal but relevant information: i.e., volunteer work that relates to your field; awards and prizes; special aptitudes such as negotiating skills, that you work well on a team (or handle large projects alone), that you welcome challenges, adapt quickly to company policies and have a clear vision of your direction … whatever you do exceptionally well that you have not included elsewhere.

Finally, your list of credentials is important. However, offering information that reveals your character and compatibility goes a long way to influence an employer to pick up the phone and call you. You just may be granted an interview instead of a candidate with more experience and qualifications than you but whose résumé lacks any personal traits.

Taking the Plunge: Searching for That Dream Job

Since you have spent time to prepare for the plunge, your search will not be as overwhelming a task as it might otherwise be. You have a head start because you already have found some places, people and prospects for your contact lists. Don't neglect checking books, magazine articles, newspaper columns and other avenues devoted to every facet about finding a job. They are loaded with information and will give your search a lift.

Here are some tips to get you started:

A valuable caveat:
Put more time off line than online because the jobs are off line.

First: Prepare a Job Search Plan

Review the tips that follow and include the suggestions in your plan, making each area as comprehensive as possible. Proceed in the way that is most comfortable for you. Review the previous section, *"Reinventing yourself,"* and make sure you have covered all the steps. There are two basic recommendations you must use and be sure you make the most of both. One, is contacting people and organizations you know ... being in touch by phone, e-mail and/or in person ... the other is networking on the Internet.

Second: Determine a Realistic Schedule

Spend an hour or two each day on your job search or whatever amount you need to be the most productive. Don't overdo it and wear yourself out. Save your energy for interviews. Establish the length of time you will work toward having a job offer. Three months, six months, more or less. If you have *not* gotten an offer by then, reassess your plan. Where should you adjust? Is it your résumé? Your attitude? Your contacts? The time you spend every day on your search? Is there a limited number of companies in your field located where you are applying? You have not included *all* the tips noted below in your plan? You have spent more time on the Internet than off line? Make the necessary changes and continue.

Third: Networking in Person is the First and Most Reliable Method

Make a list, a long list. Start with the people you know: your friends, family, neighbors, members of your church, volunteer colleagues and, if you have them, your attorney, broker, accountant, even your dentist and doctor. Expand the list to include those from your past: college

175

classmates, professors, co-workers, bosses, clients, those with whom you had contact in earlier jobs. Let them know you are in the market and for what you are qualified and hope to find.

Fourth: Networking on the Internet is Popular but Ranks Second Best

Nonetheless, it is a must and warrants your creation of a powerful presence on this medium. Studies indicate that there more than 80,000 job websites and thousands more that contain job listings. Research them and determine the ones in your field. Keep them manageable by limiting the number you spend your time on to those that have the greatest potential for you.

There are several websites that offer general information that you shouldn't overlook, such as job-hunt.org Then, discriminate by using only those websites that favor your industry when you place your profile on Twitter, Facebook, LinkedIn, VisualCV, ZoomInfo and/or Ziggs. Job openings are also listed on websites of university alumni associations, professional associations and societies (attorneys, architects, health care, banks, fashion, government, etc.), Chambers of Commerce, corporations and others.

As you proceed you will find you will be able to turn some of your website contacts into your networking-in-person contacts. To assure that your résumé is not deleted or set aside, place a call or mail a letter to confirm it was received. Your gentle persistence will show your interest in working for the company.

Visit the websites of the companies you apply to and reflect your knowledge in the cover letter that accompanies your résumé.

Fifth: Job Fairs and Virtual Job Fairs

No doubt you are aware of and have attended a job-career fair. Have you experienced a virtual job fair? Both can produce leads, but attending a fair in person draws you away from your computer and puts you face-to-face with potential employers. The typical job fair is held in a hotel, convention center and similar venues with large meeting facilities. They are sponsored by a single industry or by organizations, universities, Chambers, and others that enlist booths from companies in diverse fields. You can find them advertised in your local paper or check the Internet for events near you. Employmentguide.com is one you might check. On the other hand, virtual job fairs, or virtual career events, allow you to find employers without leaving your home. You, as the job seeker, can match your skills, experience and interests with employment opportunities by participating online. Virtual job events make the most of innovations like videos, downloadable materials, animation, webinars, live chats and social networking.

Sixth: Following Up on Your Interview

One of the most important and neglected steps in securing a job is following up each interview with a letter … whether the meeting was successful or not. (In some cases an e-mail may be appropriate.) The employer's first choice may not accept the job or may not meet his expectations. With your follow-up on his desk, (or in his computer) you may the *first* he'll call to fill the void.

Always remember to
spend more time off line than online.
Off line is where the jobs are.

Now, you are *prepared* to make your move. You are confident, ready to seek that job of your dreams. With perseverance you will be successful.

Your Own Business or a Franchise

If you choose to take the route to owning your own business or franchise, you are in another category. You are the boss, the manager, the supervisor. You will have been successful in the jobs you held in the field in which you intend to have your own company. You have the capital you need or good credit with access to borrowing, you have in-depth knowledge of the industry, you know where to locate, you have a detailed business plan and you are prepared to work ten to twelve hours a day, seven days a week.

Good luck.

Conclusion

The information in this chapter is an introduction to how you can find your dream job. However, there is enough here to get you started. Check your library, book stores and the Internet for helpful information. Talk with, and/or interview friends and professionals in your field of interest. Set a timetable and prepare a plan to ensure you make a success of your search and a proper transition and that you are fully prepared to undertake your dream job. Always keep in mind that if you are unable to sprint over hurdles along the path you've chosen, you may invest in a career coach for guidance.

CHAPTER 17

Positive Pursuits with a Purpose

*"Purpose gives you fulfillment and joy
and can bring you the experience of happiness."*

Deepak Chopra, MD,
1946-, best-selling author
and co-founder of the
Chopra Center for Wellness

Amy lost her husband in an automobile accident when she was thirty-five. She was left with two teenage girls and a boy. She remarried, had another child and lost her second husband to a heart attack when she was forty-two. She worked as a legal clerk, brought up her children, saw them married, retired to Florida. She soon became bored with beach walks, bridge and television. She finds volunteering at her church rewarding, but she needed something else, something stimulating with more of a purpose. She applied for a security officer's job in her retirement community. Amy was hired and took the required six-week course. She puts in a three-hour night tour of duty once a week for twenty-five dollars in pay. She thrives on driving the brightly lighted neighborhood streets in the official vehicle. There are few, if any, dangerous incidents, but Amy feels fulfilled and has a sense of purpose.

*There is nothing more satisfying and rewarding
than working on a project with a purpose
for yourself, for someone else, for a charity or for all three.
Or fulfill your civic duty as a political volunteer!*

Pursuits With a Purpose for Yourself

Once you have taken care of the demands brought about by the loss of your loved one and have begun a good health plan, it's time to undertake

179

a project that will bring *you* rewards. Again, you deserve it. Some are more fun than others, but the completion of the task and the results are most gratifying. You may not want a full-time job (see CHAPTER 16), but a part-time job that is easier to find – in a field that has always interested you – is a pursuit with a personal purpose. Consider being an assistant teacher, a sales clerk in an upscale boutique, a coach for kids in a sport you excel in, working in a library or behind the scenes in a theater. Whatever is your pleasure!

There are other projects closer to and at home. Is it time to redecorate your home, maybe just one room with a fresh coat of paint, another with new wallpaper or refinish the kitchen cabinets? Conquer the clutter in your closets, empty the garage … the attic … the basement. Fill your garden or the planters on your deck with flowers in your favorite colors. Take a course in gourmet cooking, an exotic subject or one to improve your computer skills. Planning and pursuing your project can be as gratifying as achieving its purpose.

The purpose is yours.
Pursue it and enjoy the results!

Pursuits with a Purpose That Help Someone Else

"The best way to cheer yourself up
is to try to cheer somebody else up."

Mark Twain, 1835-1910, pundit, author

Now that I am alone, I live in a fifty-two-unit townhouse community in a rural area interspersed with tall, venerable trees and surrounded by farms with meadows and roaming cows and sheep. I love it. Most of my neighbors are retired couples. Several still drive to work and there is only one family with children, a pair of nine-year-old twin boys. Twelve of us are single women, mostly widows and two divorcées. (Oh, yes, ten single men, no matches that I know of). Every family enjoys the privacy we all have. We have two community parties a year … Christmas and a pool party in the summer.

Some of us have become good friends and meet from time to time. Most gratifying to see is the generous help that residents, men and women, give the single women-in- need: getting their mail, shopping, driving them to a doctor's appointment, taking out and returning the trash containers and more. Recently Fran's husband died of Alzheimer's disease shortly after they moved into the community. I've come to know her. We share a great deal. When I mentioned this book I'm writing, she asked for copies of the chapters I'd completed. After reading them, she said, "I feel your book is talking directly to me ... that you understand what I am experiencing. You are helping me handle my grief. What you have written is comforting and gives me peace." Her comments confirmed that I am fulfilling "*my* pursuit with a purpose."

You won't have to go far
to find a friend, a relative, or a neighbor
who will fulfill your purpose of helping someone else.

Pursuits with a Purpose That Help Multitudes Via Charities

"Who pleasure gives shall joy receive."

Benjamin Franklin, 1706-1790,
statesman, diplomat, publisher, inventor

A positive pursuit with purpose in the broadest sense reaches out to far more people than any other. This pursuit is *volunteerism*. The causes are endless. You do not need a special talent to be a volunteer, to give help and pleasure. There are assignments available on every level, from filing, answering the phone and stuffing envelopes to organizing a fund-raiser and giving speeches on behalf of the cause. You are welcome regardless of what you have to offer. In return you will receive that special joy. It has been said that the giver often feels an even greater reward than the one who receives.

There may be a cause you have wanted to support but had never undertaken or had the time or the need to pursue. Now may be the right time. Or, if you are ready to experience that joy but would like first to learn about the categories in fields that offer opportunities in volunteerism, here are several: literacy, children's welfare, food kitchens, religious charities, conservation, disease research and assistance, wildlife preservation, adoption agencies, health care, veterans, retirees, housing for the poor, education, international relations and natural disaster relief. You will find local charities, as well as national charities with local chapters. The National Center for Charitable Statistics reports that there are 1.6

million American public charities. With that overwhelming number in our country, you may find it difficult to make a choice. However, learning about some of those out there is a good place to start.

To help you in your search, I list here three of the categories and a few of the related charities by name, with website or other contact information:

Children's charities:

UNICEF: The United Nations Children's Fund works for children's rights, their survival, development and protection around the world. unicef.org .

Toys for Tots collects and distributes new, fun and educational toys at Christmas to less fortunate children in the United States. toysfortots.org.

Special Olympics gives young athletes with intellectual disabilities the opportunity to participate in sports and other endeavors to achieve dignity and acceptance. specialolympics.org.

Reach Out and Read encourages parents of six-months to five-year-olds to read aloud to their children. ROR provides reading rooms, books and volunteer readers. reachoutandread.org.

Make-A-Wish Foundation "grants wishes to children with life-threatening medical conditions to enrich the human experience with hope, strength and joy." wish.org.

Animal Charities

Petfinder assists you in learning about adoption, pet searches, adoption group locations and classified ad placement. petfinder.com.

ASPCA: The American Society for the Prevention of Cruelty to Animals fights puppy mills, cruelty to animals, dog fighting and more. aspca.org.

Defenders of Wildlife is dedicated to preserving the nation's wildlife and their habitats ... including wolves, grizzly bears, jaguars and other mid-sized land and water carnivores. defenders.org..

Wildlife Rescue & Rehabilitation provides medical treatment and a habitat for wild, exotic and farm animals that are orphaned, injured or displaced. Many are released into the wild but some are given permanent homes in a 187-acre facility in San Antonio, Texas. wildlife-rescue.org.

PETA: People for the Ethical Treatment of Animals focuses on areas in which the largest numbers of animals suffer the most: factory farms, the clothing industry, in laboratories and the entertainment industry. PETA also works on issues that relate to cruelty to domesticated animals. peta.org.

Health-related-charities

Of the 1.6 million American public charities, about 90,000 are health-related organizations. Selecting one or more for your volunteer services can be a challenge. However, you may choose one in which you have a personal interest: a hospital that cared for a loved one, a disease that was the cause of the loss of your husband, friend or relative, or a charity that supports educational programs that benefits a young person you know.

Here are some categories, as presented by WebMD that you may research:

Medical research organizations
These centers focus on biomedical research into subjects like the disease process, immune response and the development of medications to fight diseases. They do not include patients in their studies. One such organization, of which there are many, is the Autism Research Institute.

Disease-specific charities
This group of charities includes large and small organizations that concentrate on the many types of cancers and childhood diseases. They raise funds which are contributed to research foundations. Examples of these charities are the Shriners and the Pancreatic Cancer Action Network.

Advocate charities
These charities fund mobilization of support for legislation, educational programs, screenings for prevention and training for the public and medical professionals. The American Heart Association is a well-known advocacy charity.

Hospital foundations

These foundations are fund-raising institutions that make contributions to hospitals for services, programs and equipment they otherwise may not be able to provide. St. Joseph's Foundation in Phoenix, Arizona is among the well-known foundations.

Health outreach and relief teams
These charities reach out to the poor and suffering throughout the world. During times of disaster and crises, they provide health and relief to people in dire need. There are many such teams, including the Salvation Army, the Red Cross and PATH, the Program for Appropriate Technology in Health.

For more information about health charities, check webmd.com. WebMD is a website that "provides credible information and in-depth reference materials about health subjects."

> *A caveat: Before you offer your help,*
> *check out the organization to make sure*
> *it is a qualified, registered entity.*
> *Your local Better Business Bureau is a reliable source.*

Pursuits with a Purpose in Politics

Politics may not be a charity, but it falls in the broad category of worthwhile *Positive Pursuits with a Positive Purpose.* Political parties and organizations with political and governmental objectives will welcome you with open arms as a volunteer. You may even go on and be hired for a salaried position. Taking part in any phase of our democratic process can be an exciting and a great learning experience. You will also be contributing to the operation of our country and fulfilling your civic duty.

There are several areas of opportunities to choose from: the district (ward) level, town/city level, county, state and national levels, or party or political action committees. You can work as a volunteer for a candidate running for office or in an elected official's headquarters. Whether you give a few hours a week or several every day you are appreciated. You are most needed during political campaigns, since the cost of running for office today is almost prohibitive.

Some of the volunteer positions you may be called upon to fill are:

Headquarters' office tasks: stuffing envelopes, manning the phones, collecting publicity and preparing signs

Research: the issues, the opposition candidate(s)

Phoning: calling supporters for funds, calling voters on Election Day, polling the public on which candidate they have chosen

Campaigning with the candidate: driving him/her to events, keeping him/her on schedule, prepping him/her on the venue and those attending the event

Coordinating fund-raisers: finding and working with supporters who will hold fund-raisers, hiring a caterer (or will the host/hostess supply the food), preparing the list of contributors, setting the date and locale, sending out invitations

Campaign literature: writing press releases, leaflets, programs for special events *Election Day:* acting as a challenger at the polls, driving the disabled and senior citizens to the polls

Other: contacting the media, distributing literature, posting lawn signs

To learn where you can offer your services, you may call an office holder in any level of government that interests you, or a county clerk in some areas will direct you. Working hard on a campaign is exciting and has many rewards. You will make interesting new friends, never have a dull moment … and take part in a rousing party on election-day night, whether your candidate wins or loses.

Conclusion

When you become engrossed in a *Pursuit with a Positive Purpose* you are not only reaching out to help others, you will find you are helping yourself. You will be able to set aside some of your grieving and other concerns, particularly when you become deeply involved. Knowing that someone else has benefited from your caring, you will experience a sense of joy and gratification that few other pursuits will offer. Helping others is a strong, positive undertaking that contributes to your achieving *Contentment*.

CHAPTER 18

Pleasurable Pursuits

*"Pleasure is the object, the duty
and the goal of all rational creatures."*

François Marie Arouet Voltaire,
1694-1778 French philosopher
and writer

*Y*ou owe yourself the joy of pleasurable pursuits! You may still be grieving ... if you are, you deserve a respite: an hour or two every day from the tasks of adjusting to living without your loved one. You may feel guilt even at the thought of experiencing joy. Try to set the guilt aside, and consider how you can begin to return to a "normal" life. If you feel you are ready ... all the more reason for you to pursue pleasures. Not only do you deserve to escape from your despair, philosopher **Voltaire** declares it is your duty to make pleasure your goal. You are alone now. You should make pleasure-seeking a part of your new life. Pursuing pleasures will also help you add to your circle of friends. Indulging in pleasures does not mean an all-night binge or heavy partying. Take care and start out slowly with:

*A quiet time alone at home for a great beginning.
Go on to pursuits away from home that you can enjoy by yourself.
Then to more active pleasures nearby with friends.
Follow by attending performances of the arts.
When you are ready, leave home behind and travel!*

Here are some pleasurable pursuits you may consider:

Quiet Pleasures You Can Enjoy Alone, at Home

The simplest and easiest pleasures, when you are alone, take place at home and will often bring you the most peace. They are also the most obvious. Climb into a steaming tub and feel the refreshing sensations of a fragrant bubble bath. Plunk yourself down in a comfortable chair in your living room or bedroom with a glass of wine or a cup of coffee or tea beside you and in your hands the book you have put off reading for months. Then enjoy the read. Or relax in a recliner and watch an escapist TV show or a DVD. Have you ever thought about taking up the old-fashioned crafts (they are also arts) of sewing, knitting or crocheting? I have found sewing at night in bed as I watch television a comforting diversion ... *multi-tasking.*

Try turning your kitchen into a happy venue by breathing the aromas while you cook a favorite dish just for you. Bake a pan of brownies or prepare another sinful dessert ... then savor the results! According to **Lord George Byron,** 1788-1824, the English poet and rock star of his time, *"Pleasure's a sin, and sometimes sin's a pleasure."*

Other rewarding pleasures can take place in other parts of your home: lying on a chaise or hammock on your porch or deck as you meditate, gardening in your yard, taking photos of your home and family members when they visit and arranging the pix in albums. There are tasks you have always wanted to do but never had time for, like checking your wardrobe to eliminate some outdated items, then shopping for something new; flipping through a magazine in the growing pile on your desk; organizing old photos tucked away in boxes and drawers (for the sweetness of nostalgia) ... all pleasurable.

Nearby Pleasures to Enjoy Alone

You may wish to reach out and spend time away from home, by yourself. Or you are ready to go out but everyone you know is busy with their own affairs. You hunger to leave your home for a while and put sadness aside. You are alone. No matter! You don't have to stay home ... nor go far to find myriad pleasures to experience *and* ... enjoy your own company.

Ellen lives in the suburbs with several nearby town and county parks that offer miles of hiking trails and bridle paths. One is close enough for her to walk to. She drives to others for a change of scenery. Ellen started out by walking a mile every day and over several months she increased her walks to five. One sunny day she looked into the equestrian facilities at one of the parks and decided to take lessons. Now she rides horseback several miles through the tree-lined trails two or three times a week. She continues her walking schedule on the other days.

Julie always dined out with her husband, Elliot, at least once a week. It was almost two years since he died and she had not visited a restaurant since, except on occasion with family or a friend. She felt it was time to test the waters, alone. To avoid sad memories, she selected a Spanish eatery, one that she and Elliot never tried. Though at first she was apprehensive at the thought of dining by herself, she was soon delighted. She practiced her Spanish with the friendly waiter while selecting from the extensive menu. The ambience was inviting, the food was superbly exotic and the service excellent. She wrote a review of her experience and warily offered it to a local magazine. It was accepted. To her surprise, she received a check in the mail and was asked to submit others. She did, they were approved and now she writes a monthly restaurant column. Julie is paid for her supper as she enjoys her pleasurable pursuit!

There are other pursuits to enjoy away from home, which have rewards that go beyond pure pleasure. You can take a course in a subject that you have always wanted to pursue. Studying can be fun, an exciting learning experience and can open new worlds for you. Check the local community colleges, museums, craft centers, libraries and specialty schools. They offer instruction in languages, music – both voice and instrumental training – painting, sculpture, writing, ceramics, cooking, all phases of technology and much more.

You will find more than pleasure when you seek out beautiful structures. Consider churches. They offer peace and spiritual rewards, from the small, rural, white clapboard houses of worship with hand-crafted steeples to the city cathedrals with lofty ceilings, marble floors and columns, buttresses, family chapels and exquisite stained-glass windows.

Soon after the funeral of Richard, her husband of fifteen years, *Beatrice* felt a desire and need to explore the places of worship within a few miles of her suburban community. She attended services in several, returned again and again to the first and finally became a member. It wasn't the grandest structure, nor was the congregation the largest, nor the most cosmopolitan. It was the music that inspired her ... and the friendly people! The youthful choir director plays the organ and on occasion she wheels in her harp, gently plucks its strings and fills the building with lyrical music that only that instrument can evoke. Beatrice found pleasure, joy and the spiritual peace in this country church that she did not realize she was seeking.

There are ways to find pleasure and a sense of peace at so many other places: sitting on a bench in a hillside park, watching a brilliant setting sun; wandering a path along a stream and listening to the water splash over rocks; walking your neighborhood's tree-lined streets as song sparrows dash about among the branches; strolling a sandy beach under early morning skies to the sound of white capped waves; or wherever you find *Contentment.*

Active Pleasures Nearby with and/or to Make Friends

Months, or perhaps a year or two have passed. You still have moments when you grieve for the love you lost but you finally admit that you want to move on to a more active, more involved new life. Your family and friends have encouraged you and support you in your decision. You have been alone, have come to grips with *solitude* and have found peace. You still may have lingering feelings of guilt to move on. But you finally accept that you are ready.

You are ready for more active, pleasurable pursuits. You are ready for a change of scenery. You are ready to mingle with others, to laugh, to have fun and excitement with your friends and with new ones you hope to make.

What should you look for? Where should you look?

Pursuits are numerous and they are everywhere and within easy reach.

Let's start with where you should look!

You may try the Internet; local organizations including the YWCA (or if there is not one in your community, the YMCA has programs for women); fitness and other local health and wellness centers, as well as commercial boutiques with special programs. You will be welcome as a newcomer and you will find partners and teams or groups to join. Some are just for women, others also invite men. The activities are not only pleasurable, but they often help maintain your health, keep you focused and relieve your stress.

The "Ys" and fitness and wellness centers offer physical facilities and courses. There are swimming pools, indoor walking tracks, classes in aerobics, tai chi, yoga (also see CHAPTER 6 and 7) and scores more. You are welcome to use the myriad gym equipment: treadmills, exercise machines, recumbent slides, upright bikes, workout benches, inversion therapy tables, leg extension and curl machines, rowing machines, kettlebells, barbells, air walk trainers, elliptical trainers and vertical leg presses. Select one or more that best suits you.

Another Active Pleasurable Pursuit: Dancing

> *"Dancing is a perpendicular expression*
> *of a horizontal desire!"*
>
> George Bernard Shaw,
> 1856-1950, Irish playwright

You will find a dance that will become a passion with partners and groups that will share your excitement. There are even some dances, like forms of salsa, that you can perform alone. Dance classes are held at firehouses, church extension buildings, school gyms, local pubs, ethnic community centers and mall shops and boutiques. Here are some of the dances to select from:

Ballroom dancing: waltz, foxtrot, Latin, swing, jitterbug, tango, salsa
Folk dancing: square dancing, Polish, Russian, Spanish, Irish dancing and the dance of your own ethnic heritage
Zumba: combines dance, musical overtones and a contemporary beat (see CHAPTER 6: *Your Health and Exercise.*)
Nia: labeled by its founders, Dancing Through Life, is a system that "integrates the sensations of healthy movements into every aspect of living. It is a dance that weaves sound and silence, action and inaction, and perception and reality. Its movements are based on the body's way, with limitless forms of expression."

Active pursuits can be exhilarating,
fill some of your needs for exercise
and help keep you healthy.

Take in the Arts, Alone or with a Friend

Participating in or attending performances or exhibits of the arts goes a long way toward achieving *Solitary Contentment* and/or making friends. There is nothing more pleasurable than experiencing, first-hand, the culture of our country and that of other nations.

Arts events, both visual and performing, as well as amateur and professional, are numerous, scheduled every season of the year and are near or in easy reach of your home. You will find them in most every community, from a hamlet in the Midwest, to a country village in New England, to any town or suburb in your state and, of course, the large metropolitan cities. No matter where you live, you will find live performances and organizations dedicated to holding exhibits of works by local and widely known artisans.

If you haven't yet experienced the arts, or are not aware of *all* that is available and you are ready to reach out, be prepared for delights and surprises. Your weekly and daily newspapers as well as the Internet carry listings of the cultural events in your area. Libraries, community colleges and universities are other sources of information. They also resonate as venues for exhibits and performances of regional and worldwide cultures.

If you are drawn to the visual arts, you will find an abundance that includes painting, architecture, sculpture, photography, antiques and crafts at museums and galleries. If you prefer the performing arts or include them in your pleasurable pursuits, there are the theater, cinema, ballet and all forms of dance, opera, musicals and concerts. The arts have gone on to include literature, book signings, lectures on every subject, and gastronomy into the repertoire.

Once you have become a gourmet of a particular art, you may choose to go beyond being an observer. There are premieres, before-and-after receptions and discussions to attend where you meet and get to know the artists and performers. I've made a good friend of a young baritone, *Jason,* whom I met after a George Mason University opera performance. Or you can make a difference by joining a "Friends" committee and help raise funds for your art of choice.

> *You may begin your journey in the arts alone,*
> *but you soon will be in the company*
> *of many others who share your passion.*

Travel

> *"The soul of a journey is liberty, perfect liberty,*
> *to think, to feel, to do just as one pleases!"*
>
> William Hazlitt, 1778-1830,
> English philosopher, critic, writer

The most extended-time, pleasurable pursuit ... whether you are in a group, with a companion or alone ... is to travel!

You are alone? The ways you may travel are boundless!

You may choose to join a typical tour group of couples and families, take a singles tour or a cruise that caters to both single men and women or join one of the "girls only" travel groups/clubs.

The travel industry has taken up the gauntlet and supplies you with an abundance of choices. I'll not discuss the offers for the first group ... the couples and families ... these you can review with your travel agent if that is your choice.

Since this book is for you, as a single woman, I concentrate on the other two ... singles travel for both men and women ... and "girls only." If you want to travel and have no companion to accompany you, you don't have to suffer sorrowful glances from happy couples and extended families for your "plight" of aloneness. There are loads of options and you never have to travel alone.

Travel options for groups of single men and women

Let's explore the ways you can be in the company of singles of both sexes seeking fun, attending events, experiencing fine dining and enjoying exotic adventures while traveling together. I don't promise, but there may even be a tall, dark, handsome, financially secure, eligible guy out there just right for you. It has happened. But don't count on it. You can, however, have a great vacation and make fascinating new friends. There are travel companies that cater exclusively to singles and understand what you want and are eager to fill your needs for exciting tours and cruises. Here is some of what you can expect when you book into a singles group:

> Singles of all ages from their 20s to over 60, plus specials for the same age groups
>
> Lengths from three-night weekends to a hundred and ten nights
>
> Prices in ranges from economy to luxury
>
> Same-sex roommate matching to save the single supplement charge
>
> Tour directors trained to coordinate singles travel
>
> Special events planned for your singles groups
>
> Groups in numbers from sixty to three hundred
>
> Theme travel: hiking, biking, sailing, museum hopping, nature and all sorts of adventures. Even a three-day weekend Cougar Cruise!

What you can expect on a singles cruise (in addition to the above)?

> *Size of ships:* from yachts for a hundred to large ocean liners for over three thousand guests.
>
> *Singles groups on ships:* The entire ship is *not* dedicated to singles but accommodates all passengers plus your singles group. Your group has a tour director, organized events, cocktail parties with complimentary drinks, separate singles dining areas, games, dances, mixers and more.
>
> *Costs include:* your cabin, all meals, entertainment, items listed above. Not included are alcohol and soft drinks, optional shore excursions, insurance, available transfers, personal services and gratuities.
>
> *Night before departure:* "meet and greet" at a hotel for your singles group.
>
> *Shops and casinos:* onboard the ships.
>
> *Day at sea:* You can take part in shipboard activities for all

passengers and/or those organized especially for your singles group. Or sunbathe on one of the decks and swim in the pools.

Shore excursions: Guided optional tours are available at all ports of call. Or you can saunter about on your own to explore and shop.

Cruise-Sailing Waters

Most of the singles, both men and women, with whom I've discussed singles travel indicate they most enjoy the experiences offered on cruises – traveling oceans, lakes, seas and rivers. Cruises can be booked directly through the ship lines or the websites listed in this chapter. Here are many of the waterways throughout the world that you can enjoy sailing with other singles:

The Offshore Waters and Seas
>   The West, East and Gulf coasts of the United States and Alaska
>   The west coast and the Yucatan Peninsula of Mexico
>   The Caribbean
>   The Mediterranean
>   The Black Sea
>   The fjords of Scandinavia
>   The Antarctic

The Rivers
>   The St. Lawrence River
>   The Danube
>   The Mississippi River
>   The Dnieper River
>   The rivers of France
>   The Amazon
>   The Rhine River
>   The Nile
>   The Yangtze River in China

Some websites to search for a cruise

Here are a few of the many singles websites you can check for destinations to suit you and groups to travel with:
>   singlestravelcompany.com

vacationstogo.com/singles
backroads.com
singlestravelintl.com
singlescruises.com

Now, for the "girls only" way!

If you're not yet ready to mingle with the opposite sex, you may decide to go the "girls only" way. It is yours to choose from scores of designed-for-women theme tours and cruises: spas, decorating, cooking, antiquing, bird watching, culture and history, homes and gardens, gourmet dining, vineyards and wine tasting, your favorite sport, nature adventures and so much more. The first time you find yourself ready to take that "going away alone vacation" can be overwhelming.

Louise had been widowed for three years and always planned vacations with her husband. She was eager to travel again but was hesitant. She didn't know where and how to begin the process of going it alone. One day at lunch in her company's cafeteria, she sat with *Sally,* a co-worker and a long-time widow, who mentioned the fun she had on her recent women-only tour. Louise invited Sally to her home to learn more. Happy to oblige, Sally talked enthusiastically about the several "girls only" tours and cruises she had taken. "Traveling with other single women," she said, "is more than taking in the sights. The most rewarding times are those we women spend with each other in small, intimate groups and one-on-ones, just chatting, hanging out together on the deck of a ship, on the veranda of a country inn or on the beach … away from reminders of what we face every day. We have so much in common and so much to share. We laugh, we cry, we sing, and we talk a lot. Women understand women. We exchange experiences and share how we handle our grief and move forward as we live alone. There are also the quiet times. The entire experience is comforting, helpful and empowering."

All this is possible because as single women travel they are relaxed and comfortable in "have a good time" surroundings. There is a unique camaraderie of traveling with other genial women as they meet new people, explore new places and learn about new cultures.

Sally helped Louise through the planning and booking processes and saw her off on her first "girls only" tour … to Paris. If you have never been beyond the shores of America, the capital of France is a great place to start. That city can be the beginning of your theme tour travels. You can visit the rest of the capitals of Europe, then follow with countries on the other continents … or develop theme tours of your own.

You don't have to rely on a relative or friend to help you sign up for your "girls' only" travel experience. Check one or more of the websites listed here, locate a phone number and request a representative. They are all helpful and will make certain you connect with the tour or cruise that you seek:

just-the-girls.com
callwild.com
industravels.ca/wow-tours.html: Women Only Worldwide
adventurouswench.com/trips
destinationspavacations.com
womens-travel.gordonsguide.com
gutsywomentravel.com
great-womens-vacations.com
adventurewomen.com

For the much traveled single

You have traveled most of your life. You are a sophisticated wanderer. But it has been months or perhaps years since you lost your loved one and had a vacation. You need to get away … do you want the calm of opulent, vintage surroundings of resorts in the United States or are you ready for an exotic, absorbing, fast-paced getaway someplace on the other side of the world?

Let's explore the first: More than likely you choose to be alone, somewhere that is spiritual and relaxing, where you can renew your sense of resiliency and confidence. Someplace luxurious where you can be pampered and enjoy solitude when you please and the company of others if you wish. Resorts where the views are breathtaking and the establishments elegant and historic.

There are old-time classic destinations in the United States that have been host to presidents, celebrities, the rich and the famous. Most have been renovated, are available at somewhat reasonable off-season rates and are ready to welcome you. Indulge yourself for a weekend, a week or longer if you have the time and the wherewithal to afford it.

You may consider:

The Point at Saranac Lake, New York ... a dog-friendly retreat that offers elegant cathedral-ceiling suites. Activities include ice skating, snow barbeques, cross-country skiing, boating, campfire cookouts and Saturday black-tie dinners.

The Homestead, Hot Springs, Virginia ... dates back to 1766 and was expanded in the early 20th century with sprawling red brick buildings flanking a multi-story structure and clock tower. Hosted the Astors, DuPonts, Windsors and more. Winter and summer sports, including carriage rides, bowling, classes in falconry, plus the healing waters of natural springs.

Greystone Castle Sporting Club, Mingus, Texas ...near the Dallas/ Fort Worth airport, is the resort you cannot ignore if you love wide open spaces, wildlife and the luxury of a medieval castle set in the midst of six thousand enchanting acres. Hunt or prey-stalk sable, wildebeest, ibex, zebra, nyala ... and duck, quail, partridges and pheasant. Relax in the steaming hot tub or take a dip in the pool.

Omni Mount Washington Resort, Bretton Woods, New Hampshire ... offers its spectacular Canopy Tour, a series of suspension bridges and zip lines that takes three-and-a-half hours to cover and descends a thousand feet of mountainside along the roof of the woodlands. The White Mountains are the backdrop for the imposing, renovated, two-hundred room, Spanish Renaissance landmark structure. Lots of snow for winter sports and sun for golf and summer sports.

Mohonk Mountain House, New Paltz, New York ... a rambling Victorian-style Alpine chalet, sits high on the rocky Shawangunk Ridge. An affordable rate includes meals, afternoon tea and activities: horseback riding, hiking along miles of trails, boating, fishing and swimming in the private, half-mile-long lake.

Now to the second, the exotic, fast-paced getaways: You are physically fit and seek something challenging and a grand distraction. Perhaps something extravagant. You feel you deserve it, no doubt you do, and you can afford to indulge yourself. Here are just a few to contemplate:

The Island of Robinson Crusoe, Chile: Repeat an historic adventure to this small island, the inspiration for the novel. Take a two-hour flight west in a seven-seater plane from Santiago, Chile's capital, and a short speedboat ride to San Juan Bautista for snorkeling and a view of a hundred-year-old shipwreck.

Mongolia: Fly to the other side of the globe to Ulaanbaatar, the capital of Mongolia, and visit its museums and temples. Continue your flight to Gobi and explore the desert by camel and jeep; meet nomadic reindeer herders and take in the expanse of Lake Khövsgöl, the country's vast fresh water lake.

Ngamba: a one-hundred-acre island of rainforests supporting a diversity of wildlife, located near the equator and a fifty-minute boat ride from Entebbe.

Uganda: Visitors can view chimpanzee feedings at a unique chimpanzee sanctuary and enjoy eco-friendly facilities with spacious luxury tents.

Dubai: a city and emirate located south of the Persian Gulf on the Arabian Peninsula, is the grandest, most modern and fastest growing Arab tourism destination. You can enjoy luxurious skyscraper hotels, splendid shopping malls, miles of the whitest, sandiest beaches, water sports, an indoor snow center for skiing and snowboarding, a camel racetrack, a desert safari, "a few sinful pleasures" and much, much more. Dubai is a city-state to visit at least once in a lifetime.

Mustique: a fourteen-hundred-acre private island sanctuary in the West Indies, one of a group called the Grenadines … with natural, tropical vegetation, several coral reefs and nine pristine beaches. There are a hundred elegant villas, a health spa, an equestrian center, a tennis club and renowned Basil's Beach Bar. Be sure not to miss the mule trip around the island.

Conclusion

The world abounds with pleasurable pursuits that will help fulfill your goal of *Solitary Contentment* … pursuits for you to experience alone or with others. I have presented several possibilities in this chapter, more than enough, and perhaps too many from which to choose. To help you decide, I suggest that first you review the sections (listed below and at the opening of this chapter), then select the one – or more if you can handle them – that define(s) where you are and where you want to be.

Quiet times alone at home
Pursuits away from home, alone
Nearby active pleasures with friends
Attending the arts alone or with others
Leave home and travel

Once you have made your decision, research your choice … on the Internet, in the library, book stores, magazines, newspapers … then actively *pursue your pleasurable pursuits.*

CHAPTER 19

Pack Up and Move

"Taking a new step, uttering a new word
is what people fear most."

Fyodor M. Dostoyevsky,
1821-1891, Russian writer

"To live is to change, and to be perfect
is to have changed often."

John Henry Newman, 1801-1890,
British prelate and writer

*I*f you are thinking of moving from your current home, take your first step by reading and/or re-reading CHAPTER 5: *A Cautionary Tale: Go Slowly. Set Goals. Have a Plan.* Make sure you have met all the recommended criteria before you proceed.

This chapter offers you a list of factors you should consider as you plan your move along with a few suggestions as to where you might choose to live ... here in the United States, as well as places in other countries around the world.

Fyodor Dostoyevsky warns you, ***John Henry Newman*** challenges you. It is up to you to weigh all the criteria and make the final decision. The most critical determination is ... *are you ready ... are you emotionally, physically and financially prepared?*

Moving is a major event in anyone's life. Making the change now that you are *alone* is more challenging than it would have been with your significant other by your side. Do you feel up to handling all the factors wisely and devoting the necessary time to each? Will you be able to make sound decisions to achieve a smooth transition from your current lifestyle to a new one?

The journey can be exciting and a distraction from your loss.
The destination can open the door
to new experiences, adventures and relationships.

It was eight years after my husband died. I felt very much alone and ready to make the move. I was fortunate to have someone help me through the conditions, step by step. She was Daisy, my real estate agent, who has become a best friend. She studied my situation, researched the market and found the perfect townhouse for me in a community of friendly neighbors with values much like mine. I am settled in and could not be happier with my new home and to have made the move when I did.

Factors to Consider Before Making Your Move

Writing down the answers to most or all of the following questions will help you decide whether you are ready to make a move and stir your thoughts on developing a plan if you are. I list these factors in the form of questions for they are very personal and only you can make the determinations:

1. *Why do you want to move now? Are your reasons valid? Are you prepared for the myriad tasks to make your move and to leave longtime friends behind and make new ones?*

2. *When do you want to have completed your move?*

3. *Where in the world do you want to live and why?*

4. *What type of property will you look for? A single-family house, a condominium, a townhouse, an apartment? Which best fits your lifestyle?*

5. *How is your health? Can it handle the move? What health-care facilities are available in the area where you plan to move?*

6. *What kind of weather and climate suits you?*

7. *Have you sold your current dwelling? Have you analyzed your finances? Do you have a budget for the move? Can you afford it?*

8. *Do you want to live in a city, suburb, the country, a small community?*

9. *Have you compared the real estate and sales and state tax rates to what you are paying now?*

10. *Have you checked the area's statistics for violent crimes and vandalism?*

11. *Do you want to purchase a home or rent? If you buy, are you prepared to make necessary improvements? Do you have the time and money to do so?*

12. *Do you want the friendliness of a little town or the excitement and sophistication of a big city?*

13. *Does the area where you plan to move meet your criteria for lifestyle, cultural events and your interests and hobbies?*

14. *Have you visited the area during the summer and winter seasons to assure that it offers what you are looking for ... that you can adjust and will be happy and comfortable there?*

15. *If you are downsizing, are you taking an inventory of what to discard before your move and what to take? Are your furnishings suitable for your new home?*

16. *If you have one or more pets, have you checked the regulations for transporting them to and having them live in your new home?*

17. *Have you negotiated with more than one reliable mover to get the best job and the best deal?*

18. *Should you seek the advice of a financial adviser and a real estate agent?*

Julie came out of a bitter divorce with a good financial settlement and decided to buy a house that was much smaller than the one she left. That was wise. She rushed and bought a charming Cotswold-style cottage on an acre of land in need of a great deal of repair. A red flag! She spent three years agonizing while she had the utilities replaced and the grounds landscaped. When she began to redesign the interior she was drained and exhausted. Julie realized she had been hasty in buying her new home. Besides being worn out, she had little time to spend on her volunteer work and visiting with her adult children. Luckily, her *charming cottage* quickly attracted a buyer and she moved into a newly built townhouse village where the rooms of her unit were freshly painted and papered with colors and designs of her choice and the grounds are maintained by the homeowners association's landscapers. Julie says she regrets she was unaware of the list of factors before her first move. She would have spent more time planning to relocate.

Giving thought to the factors' questions and answering them honestly can save you time, money and heartache over the long run and help you find Solitary Contentment.

Looking for a Big City with a High Quality of Life

According to the Mercer* Quality of Life Report, the city with the best living standard among all the cities in the world is Vienna, Austria. Within the top thirty, there are seven German cities, four in Canada and Australia, three in Switzerland, two in the United States ... *Honolulu and San Francisco* ...with one or two in the rest of countries on the list.

The German cities are Munich, Düsseldorf, Frankfurt, Hamburg, Nuremberg and Berlin. The Canadian cities are Vancouver, Ottawa, Toronto and Montreal. The Australian cities are Sydney, Melbourne, Perth and Canberra. The Swiss cities are Zurich (which ranks second after Vienna), Geneva and Berne.

Mercer evaluates living conditions in four hundred and twenty cities. The conditions are grouped in ten categories: political/social environment, economic environment, socio-cultural environment, health and sanitation, schools and education, public services and transportation, recreation, consumer goods, housing and the natural environment. Though the research and analyses are thorough, Mercer disclaims any warranties. Should any of the cities interest you, you may visit the Internet for more information.

*Mercer, mercer.com, a worldwide consulting and investment management firm with 20,000 employees in 40 countries, is a wholly owned subsidiary of Marsh & McLennan Companies, Inc.

Some Places to Consider in the United States:

You are ready to pack up and move! You have analyzed your answers to the moving conditions and you've determined to settle within the United States. A great place for your new home is in your own state, your own county, even your own community. The adjustments you will have to make will be few ... you can attend the same church, shop in the same supermarket and malls, visit the same hairdresser, call on the same plumber, electrician, repairman, see the same doctor and dentist and party with the same friends.

I made two moves with my husband to other areas in our state and a third to Virginia. When I made my last move, *alone,* it was not only in my own state, New Jersey, it was in the same community. My adjustments were minimal. New Jersey is a state you may choose to research. Since it is mine, I'll tout it. (I was its Director of Travel and Tourism for almost eight years and was responsible for its successful slogan, *New Jersey and You: Perfect Together.*) Every state has its positives and negatives and New Jersey is no exception, but the positives outweigh the negatives. Some of them include: one-hundred-and-twenty-seven miles of beaches, fresh water lakes, forested mountains, meadows and farmland, horse country, a plethora of upscale and fast-food restaurants, scores of discount malls, professional performing and visual arts venues, proximity to New York City and Philadelphia, affordable homes and townhouse/condominium villages, once high-priced estate properties now available at reduced prices and ... important if you are a baby boomer ... desirable retirement communities with units starting at $60.000. However, if you decide to settle in the Garden State, make sure you double check the real estate taxes on the property you plan to buy ... one of the state's few negatives. On the positive side, food and clothing are not taxed.

Other desirable move-to communities in the United States

If you favor a warm-weather climate, **Honolulu** should be at the top of your list. According to MoneyRates.com columnist, **Richard Barrington,** Hawaii is a paradise with monthly temperatures averaging from 73 degrees in January and February to 82 in August. Another plus is the life expectancy of its residents – 80 years – the longest of any state. However, check your financial situation carefully. Hawaii's cost of living is the highest at 167 percent of the national average. If you can't afford to live there and you want to experience the Hawaiian climate, book an economy islands tour and enjoy the sun and the beaches for a week or two.

*A note about affordability: As you plan your finances,
keep in mind the states that have no income taxes.
They are Alaska, Florida, Nevada, South Dakota,
Texas, Washington and Wyoming.
New Hampshire and Tennessee tax only interest and dividends.*

If you still insist on a warm climate but need something more affordable, try Florida or California. **Fort Myers,** a city with a population of 63,000 on the **Gulf Coast of Florida**, is worth checking. Its July temperatures are from 74 degrees to 92; for January they range from 54 to 75 degrees. Small homes and some condos can be found from the low $100,000 to a high of $300,000 and offer golf, clubhouses and pools. However, homes along the back bay and others on the Gulf are selling for $300,000 up to one- and two-million dollars. Real estate taxes are reasonable, there is no estate or inheritance tax. Keep in mind Florida is one of the states with no state income tax. The city boasts several boulevards lined with stately royal palms, an historic downtown district, art galleries, theaters, sidewalk cafés, and, of course, the beaches.

Then there is also semi-tropical **Melbourne, on Florida's East Coast** which also offers affordability. The temperatures range from 72 to 91 degrees in July and 50 to 72 degrees in January. Melbourne is a quiet, laid-back community with open, uncrowded beaches and outdoor sports that include kayaking, boating, surfing, fishing, tennis and golf. Nature lovers are drawn to the Florida Tech Botanical Gardens and the Brevard Zoo. From their porches and yards, residents have spectacular views of takeoffs from the Kennedy Space Center, which is only thirty miles north of the town. Disney World is an easy, sixty-mile drive from Melbourne.

California has several inviting, warm climate areas. One to consider is **Coachella Valley,** a forty-five-mile-long valley located within a bevy of mountain ranges, 105 miles southeast of Los Angeles and a few miles northwest of San Diego. Temperatures range from moderate to hot … January has 44-degree temperatures to 70; July, from 76 to 108. The valley offers scenic beauty, clear fresh air, hiking trails, dramatic views, the arts, entertainment and designer shopping malls. There are three university campuses, advanced medical facilities, including the noted Betty Ford Center for addiction treatment and condo communities with pools, fitness centers, tennis courts, golf courses and clubhouses. You will find single-family houses that are priced from the mid- $100,000s to $400,000 in the quiet, residential desert towns.

There are scores of other affordable warm-weather cities and towns throughout the United States. You will find them in Georgia, Arizona, Mississippi and the rest of the southern states.

If you are looking for scenic grandeur, cool, fresh air, casual living, a change of seasons, a mountain community, outdoor activities and winter sports, be sure check out **Bozeman, Montana.** This one-time frontier city with a college-town atmosphere is in the southwest corner of the state near the northern entrance to Yellowstone National Park. (Most of the park lies south in Wyoming.) Temperatures range from 14 to 33 degrees in January and 52 to 82 in July. Though a relatively small town with a population under 40,000 – where you can walk almost everywhere and enjoy great shopping – Bozeman has a big-city infrastructure. Public transportation and health-care facilities are exceptional. Among its many professional cultural venues are vibrant orchestral, opera and theater companies that feature acclaimed artists from around the country. Housing varies from historic properties in downtown priced from $275,000 to $1 million to a nearby planned development of maintenance-free, single-family homes that start in the high $300,000s. Others can be found in surrounding areas for similar prices. New homes in a community west of the city can be purchased for $199,000 to $300,000.

Before you make your final decision on a mountain community, you may want to check out another. *Cedar City* in southwestern *Utah* is smaller, with a population under 29,000 and is nestled among spectacular red rock canyons and foothills covered with juniper (not cedar) trees and pinyon. Also a college town, Cedar City's Southern Utah University offers a full roster of cultural and sports events for residents. The climate is diverse, with sunny days and temperatures up to 90 degrees in July and as low as 17 in January, with as much as 45 inches of snow. An abundance of recreational activities include skiing, horseback riding, hiking, cycling, kayaking, the Utah Shakespeare Festival and Groovefest, an annual event of music, food and arts and crafts. The glitter, gambling and nightlife of Las Vegas is only one-hundred-and-seventy-five miles south. Cedar City's cost of living is below average. Housing is affordable. Building tracts start at $20,000. Homes in need of some repair go for $60,000 and up. New, upscale single-family homes in one community start at $170,000. A few others are at the high end of $700,000 and more. The average, however, for a three-bedroom home is about $250,000.

So, You've Decided to Live Abroad!

Though you should answer the factors' questions no matter where you plan to move, here are more if your choice is to live in another country. Again, be as honest as you can with your answers.

1. *Will you visit the country of your choice at least two or three times, interview other Americans who live there (if there are any) and hire a local attorney?*

2. *Are you prepared to handle the different pace of life, the inefficiencies and legal ramifications unique to the country?*

3. *Are you somewhat fluent in the language of the country or ready to learn it?*

4. *Can you handle being away from family and close friends for long periods of time and pursue travel-related costs, time and difficulties for them to visit?*

5. *Are you prepared to be surrounded by natives of the country with few if any American neighbors?*

6. *Can you give up foods, cultural events (American films) not available in your new country and books, newspapers, magazines and television in English?*

If you answer yes to most or all of the above, continue to learn about some of the exciting and desirable places to move to around the world.

Let's start with *France* ... this European country has everything you could possibly want in a new location: great climate, great food, great wines, meandering roads through peaceful countrysides, sleepy villages, rolling hills, the snow-capped Alps, sunny beaches, vineyards, the arts, culture, medieval towns, chateaus and the glitter and sophistication of *Paris.* All this can be affordable if you take time to research and explore

... an enjoyable task ... and there are scores of professionals to assist you! You may find a small stone cottage in a hamlet or an enchanting hillside retreat for around $100,000 or a rambling farmhouse in need of repair for even less. If you must have Paris, and you are lucky, you may discover a pied-à-terre or a tiny walk-up on the third or fourth floor in one of the outlying arrondissements for $250,000. Not to worry, travel by métro takes you quickly and at little expense to all the attractions, including the Eiffel Tower and the Louvre. If you choose an apartment in the center of the capital city, be prepared to pay for its glamour, its history, its ambience, its antiquity, its beauty, its grace. Prices start at around $500,000 and reach high into the millions. I wish I could afford Paris!

There are other European countries, those in the southern part of the continent, where thousands of Americans choose to make their new homes. The climate, for the most part, is the main reason for their attraction ... long summers, from April through September ... except for the mountainous regions ... and delightful autumns. Winters are cool but mild, with occasional rain and wind. The ambience in these countries ... *Italy, Spain, Greece and its islands, Portugal, Malta and Croatia* ... is similar, yet each has its own distinctive style. They all offer antiquities, palazzos, cathedrals, museums, winding rural roadways, picturesque villages, vineyards, wines, boutiques, sidewalk cafés, fine restaurants, the arts, beaches, mountain resorts and all you might expect from the regions of southern Europe. Housing costs in rural areas range from under $100,000 to $300,000 with a median price of $200,000. As in Paris, the cost of living and housing in the capitals and large cities will cost you much more, but with time, effort and a little luck you may find an apartment you can afford. In a major city, you are able to walk to attractions, shopping and restaurants and take advantage of the superb European railway system to visit the rest of the country and the continent.

If you are looking for a tropical paradise like Hawaii, but without the high costs, consider the towns and villages of *Costa Rica,* which has the highest standard of living, education and health-care in Central America. *Grecia* is a mountain community in the midst of coffee and sugar plantations and cattle farms. The living pace is slow, the temperatures range comfortably from 65 to 85 degrees year round and the Mercado, the Spanish market, has a pretty church and a park lined with shade trees. A world-class hospital is thirty minutes away in San Jose and health coverage (for everything) is $45 a month for residents. (Other modern facilities are located throughout the country.) Large building lots are available for $30,000 and a three-bedroom house with two patios and furnishings made by local artisans costs $179,000. In deeply rural areas, simple, rustic but livable houses can be bought from $25,000 to $75,000 for a small charmer. The Pacific and Gulf beaches offer high-priced properties, but there are also many lovely, modest homes in the coastal communities. Though performing and visual arts venues are limited, the world-class Costa Rica National Symphony Orchestra performs in a beautiful, historical theater for only $5 a ticket. You can take a tour of Costa Rica, enjoy a vacation and learn for yourself if this paradise is right for you.

The two countries that border the United States are the top of the list of move-to countries. *Mexico,* to the south, is the most desired; *Canada,* to the north is a close second. They attract, no doubt, because they are in easy reach and offer what most movers seek … temperate climate and affordability.

Let's first look into Mexico. Why does this country have such a high influx of Americans when it has such a large presence of drug-related crime and violence … with constant coverage by the media? Strange? These are problems, big problems. The reason so many Americans select Mexico is that the crimes are confined mainly to the northern part of the country and along our border states. They choose the regions that are far from the troubled areas, regions that abound with tropical paradises … where they can live on or near the beach or rent a two-bedroom, two-bath apartment for around $400 per month and the cost of living is from $1,000 to $1,500 per month. However, there are upscale areas where the monthly living costs range from $1,700 to $3,500 depending on the type of home and lifestyle you choose. Though the climate has great appeal, if you do not thoroughly research the region you select, you may suffer from the heat and humidity during June through September and from the rain during the wet season.

Among the most sought-after areas is ***Puerto Vallarta,*** on the Pacific Coast west of Guadalajara and home to one of the largest American communities. It boasts a charming 16th-century town center, high-rise hotels, condos and time-share complexes, as well as American-brand shops, modern supermarkets and vast, palm-fringed beaches. The weather is a major attraction, with pleasurable winters and coastal breezes cooling the hot and humid summers. Other popular areas include the cities of San Miguel de Allende, Mérida in The Yucatàn, Mazatlàn and the state of Oaxaca.

Now to *Canada,* which, along with Australia and Norway, is ranked by the United Nations as one of the five most desirable countries to live in. The country is vast, the second largest (inhabited) in the world after Russia. The population is thirty-four million compared to three-hundred-and-ten million in the U.S. and offers an endless rugged wilderness along with vibrant, cosmopolitan cities. You need not travel oceans to experience exotic or European cultures. At most border crossings from the United States into Canada, there is little or no noticeable difference in lifestyles. As you move further into and around the country you'll find a fascinating blend of cultures ... French, English, Chinese, Korean and Inuit. The exchange rate is far more favorable than the euro and the laws and customs are similar to the U.S. The average temperature in the populated areas is 50 degrees and the range in summers is from 80 to 90 degrees.

Canada's attractions are diverse ... among them are summer and winter outdoor sports, blue-ribbon gardens, the arts, fine dining, festivals, boutiques, pubs and spas. With its snow-capped mountains, British Columbia is the only province that offers its West Coast Special of skiing and golf in the same day. *Whistler,* a city in the province, has the largest ski area in North America and four championship golf courses surrounded by wildflowers and pine trees. The pace in the cities that are clustered in southwest British Columbia ... including *Vancouver, Victoria and Penticton* ... is slower and more relaxed in contrast to those in the East. The cities that are on or near the Atlantic ... *Montreal, Kingston, Charlottetown and Toronto, further inland* ... hum with vibrancy and energy, have one or more universities and are seeped in history, with architecture and traditions of England and France.

Housing costs vary widely depending on location and amenities. You will find a two-bedroom apartment in Kingston for about $146,000 and those in Vancouver that run from $200.000 to $1 million. On the other hand, three-bedroom houses in Charlottetown, the capital of Prince Edward Island, range from $90,000 to the low $200,000s. In addition, the cost of living is more affordable.

Next, consider **Puerto Rico** – though a territory of the United States, it maintains the flavor and essence of Europe, brought by invaders who journeyed from Spain during the fifteenth and sixteenth centuries. A tropical island in the Caribbean, one-and-a-half times the size of Delaware, Puerto Rico is a thousand miles southwest of Miami. English and Spanish are the official languages, but Spanish pervades throughout the rural areas. The island has been modernized with American infrastructure, condo communities and shopping malls. The mountainous scenery is spectacular. There are long stretches of white sandy beaches and quaint villages in the countryside. Outdoor activities abound ... hiking on paths to the peak of El Yunque, golf on renowned courses, swimming, sport fishing and colorful festivals. In the capital of **San Juan,** you will find art galleries, boutiques, upscale restaurants, duty-free shops and night spots that vibrate to the sounds of jazz, salsa and bomba. The streets are paved with cobblestone and a five-hundred-year old stone wall circles the city. Housing costs in the countryside start from $150,000 for a three-bedroom apartment to the mid-$200,000s and higher for two bedroom condos and single-family homes with sea views. Luxury homes on golf courses in **Dorado** start at the high $300,000s with building lots available from $50,000. A plus for senior Americans who live in this island paradise is that you are covered by Medicare. Not so if you live in countries outside the United States and its territories.

Conclusion

Investing quality time when you undertake a move, whether near to your current home, somewhere else in the United States or abroad, can save you heartache and money in the long run. You will be able to enjoy, worry-free, the dream home in the paradise you have always wanted ... the sunny, warm climate of the tropics, the scenic grandeur of snow-capped mountains or the sophistication of a big city.

Though you may not need to answer all of the *criteria questions* because you know instinctively what you want and what is best for you, giving thought to them will help you avoid pitfalls. If you choose to stay in the United States, you can gain additional information by contacting the Chamber of Commerce, the real estate association and the tourism bureau in the state of your next home. Planning to move abroad? It's wise to reach out to the U.S. State Department and the American embassy in the country that interests you as well as other agencies in the nation that offer residency data and assistance.

Obviously, this chapter covers only a few places in the United States and abroad for you to consider. I hope they will inspire you to explore some of the hundreds more here in the U.S. and around the world. Many of these are referenced in the books and publications listed in suggested reading in CHAPTER 22.

Note: The housing costs included with the move-to places in this chapter were those available at the time this book was written. It is wise to double-check **all costs, taxes and related details** when you are ready to buy.

*Seeking your Shangri-La can be an exciting adventure
and help you find Contentment!*

CHAPTER 20

Conclusion

Though my book is at its end, *you* may be at the beginning of your journey in *Finding Solitary Contentment* … or you have already started.

Have you read every chapter, just a few, or have you flipped through all the pages and still wonder which chapters will put you on the path to renewal? Try turning back to CHAPTER 2 and, if you still must … grieve and cry long and often. Just remember Billy Graham's caveat: *"We just need to guard against making this … grieving … our only response, for it's not healthy."* Then, continue through the rest of the chapter. Move forward slowly, spending as much time as you need on each procedure. When you sense you are ready, go on to the rest of the chapters of *Part One*. Concentrate on the steps that will best prepare you for one or more of the new life options in *Part Two*.

How long it takes to achieve emotional and physical renewal, along with financial stability, is different for everyone. If you are spending more time than you expected on *Part One* and are having trouble moving on, you may reach out for professional assistance. You will find lists of people and organizations to guide you in CHAPTER 21.

As you pursue your adventures, you may find it helpful to return to *Part One* to repeat the suggestions that build your strengths and enable you to embrace your new life with confidence.

Researching and writing this book has been, for me, a gratifying and uplifting experience. Most rewarding is knowing that I have helped women who are alone and that my work will continue to benefit others who have lost their loved ones. Among friends and colleagues who have gained solace from reading sections of my in-progress manuscript was Fran about whom I write in CHAPTER 17. She had just lost her

215

husband of fifty-five years and told me, "I feel your book is talking directly to me." A sense of peace for her and gratifying for me

I have also taken some of my own advice by including a new companion in my life. I have adopted an elegant, intelligent six-year-old whippet. *Niqui*, for Dominique, is always at my side, joins me on my daily, two-mile morning walks and rests on the floor under my desk as I work at my computer. Niqui gives me *unconditional love*.

As I worked on my manuscript, *my pursuit with a purpose,* I discovered I was enjoying an unexpected reward. I made more than valuable contacts ... I was making new friends with the experts you find throughout my book. Though our encounters were brief (several longer than others) these friends graciously permitted me to quote or reference areas of their expertise which validate my recommendations. You will find them credited in the *Acknowledgements.*

While you are handling your grief, achieving renewal and undertaking one or more of the new life options, you may begin to realize and accept why you have been left alone. During my research and interviews with the bereaved and the experts, *I* have come to understand why.

I have expanded my view of the wonders of the world ... glorious places, fascinating people, exciting new adventures ... and I enjoy them. I have learned I have a purpose to fulfill ... and I am carrying out that resolve by reaching out to help others.

If you have not yet found your "pursuit with a purpose"
nor achieved Contentment, you will.
It is just a matter of dedication and time!

Appendix

CHAPTER 21

Resources for Further Help and Guidance

CHAPTER 1: *How Content Are You With Your Solitude?*

CHAPTER 2: *The First Hurdle: The Shock and the Grief*

RENEW: Center for Personal Recovery
(859) 756-3519

Widowed Information and Consultation
Services
(206) 241-5650

Joyce Brothers, Ph.D.
Licensed Psychologist
(615) 261-4000

John Dickerson, ED.D
Private Practice Psychologist
Belvidere, NJ
(908) 475-8100

Kevin Hoagland, Surrogate
Middlesex County Surrogate's Court
New Brunswick, NJ
(732) 745-3055

Anneli Rufus, Author
anneli@annelirufus.com

Beverly Zagofsky, MS, LPC
Licensed Family/Marriage Counselor
Chester, NJ
(908) 879-2222

GriefNet.org

Grieving.com

HelpGuide.org

HopeUnit.org

OpenToHope.com

WidowNet.org

CHAPTER 3: *Are You Prepared for Your New Life? Your Life Alone?*

Serge Kaftal, MD., FAAFP
Bernardsville, NJ
(908) 766-1223

CHAPTER 4: *Have an Identity Crisis? Learn How to Get to Know Yourself*

CHAPTER 5: *A Cautionary Tale. Go Slowly. Set Goals. Have a Plan*

CHAPTER 6: *Your Health and Exercise*

American Academy of Sleep Medicine
(630) 737-9700

The Mayo Clinic
(800) 446-2279

Mary Alldian, Pilates Instructor
Hunterdon Health and Wellness Center
(908) 735-6884

FitnessDay.com

HealthyWomen.org

WHealth.org

CHAPTER 7: *Handling Stress:*
Create "My Place" for Meditation and Relaxation

American Bando/Burmese Association
AmericanBandoAssociation.com

American Zen Association
(504) 525-3533

Foundation for International
Spiritual Unfoldment
(877) 747-4267

Harvard Medical School
(617) 432-1000

Harvard Mind/Body Institute
(617) 643-6090

Herbert Benson, MD.
Associate Professor of Medicine
mindbody@partners.org
(610) 643-6090

Carolyn Geiger, Yoga Instructor
Hunterdon Health and Wellness Center
Clinton, NJ
(908) 735-6884

ABC-Of-Yoga.com/pranayama/advanced/
bhastrika.asp

EgyptianYoga.com

FreeMeditations.com

MeditationSociety.com/108meds.html

Project-Meditation.org

TM.org/meditation-techniques/

CHAPTER 8: *Be Kind to Me Day*

CHAPTER 9: *A Great New Look*

Women's Institute of Cosmetic
and Laser Surgery
(800) 333-9243

Leslie Bauman, MD
Dermatologist
(305) 532-5552

Angela Berard, Public Relations
American Podiatric Medical Association
Bethesda, MD 20814
(301) 581-9227

Sharon Kornstein, AICI, CIP
ImageDesign LLC
(973) 740-8767

Donna Zahn, Reflexologist
Certified Massage Therapist
Califon, NJ
chloefin@aol.com

BeautyRevival.com.au

CHAPTER 10: *Face Your Sexuality Head On*

AARP
(888) 687-2277

Alan Altman, MD.
Sexual Dysfunction Specialist
Aspen, CO
(970) 925-8005

WomensHealth.gov

WomensHealthMag.com

Suki Hanfling, Sex Therapist
Belmont, Massachusetts
(617) 489-7592

Xenia Montenegro, Ph.D.
Tam Lead/Senior Research
AARP

Gina Ogden, PhD, LMFT
Certified Sex Therapist
(617) 491-0603

CHAPTER 11: *Financial Security*

Richard Barrington, CFA
Senior Financial Analyst
pr@moneyrates.com

Jerry Lynch,
Certified Financial Planner
(973) 439-1190

MoneyRates.com

Financial-Independence.com

FirstFinancialSecurity.com

FSCOnTheWeb.com

FinancialSecurityGroup.net

CHAPTER 12: *Ready for Someone New? A Significant Other?*

Lisa Diamond, Ph.D.
Psychology Professor at University of Utah
(810) 585-7491

CHAPTER 13: *Looking for a New Type of Relationship? A Woman Friend, Companion, or Lover, or a Male Confidant?*

GirlfriendSocial.com.

CHAPTER 14: *Consider a Younger Significant Other*

AgelessLove.com

AgeRomance.com

MindTheAgeGap.com

YoungerLover.com

CHAPTER 15: *Unconditional Love, a Pet*

American Kennel Club
(212) 696-8200

Best Friends Animal Society
(435) 644-2001

Deborah Cronin, VMD.
Califon Animal Hospital
Califon, NJ
(908) 832-7523

David Niven, Ph.D.
Psychologist and Social Scientist
david@davidniven.com

Joan Lowell Smith
Animal Columnist
Star Ledger
(888) 782-7533

Animal.Discovery.com/pet-planet/pet-picker

HelpGuide.org/life/pets.htm

PetChoice.org

CHAPTER 16: *Your Dream Job*

Mark Schnurman, Career Coach
(973) 452-4558

DreamJobCoaching.com

CHAPTER 17: *Positive Pursuits with a Purpose*

PathwaytoHappiness.com/pursuit_happiness.htm

CHAPTER 18: *Pleasurable Pursuits*

Singles Travel Company
cruisestoursinfo@aol.com

BestSingleTravel.com

IndependentTraveler.com

SinglesTravelINTL.com

Travel.Meetup.com

CHAPTER 19: *Pack Up and Move*

BestPlaces.net (US)

FindUtopia.com (US)

GettingOutofAmerica.com

Relocation.com

CHAPTER 22

Suggested Reading

CHAPTER 1: *How Content Are You With Your Solitude?*

CHAPTER 2: *The First Hurdle: The Shock and the Grief*

Alberti, Robert, and Bruce Fisher. *Rebuilding When Your Relationship Ends* (3rd ed.). Atascadero, CA: Impact Publishers, Inc., 2005.

Caine, Lynn. *A Compassionate, Practical Guide to Being a Widow.* New York: Penguin Group, 1990.

Manfred, Erica, and Tina B. Tessina. *He's History, You're Not: Surviving Divorce After 40.* Guilford, CT: Globe Pequot Press, 2009.

McNally, Shirley Reeser. *When Husbands Die.* Santa Fe, NM: Sunstone Press, 2005.

Moro, Ruth. *Death, Grief, and Widowhood: Experiences in Pain and Growth.* Berkeley, CA: Parallax Press, 1979.

Nowak, Pat. *The ABC's of Widowhood: A Guide to Life after a Death.* Bloomington, IN. Author House, 2003.

Oberlin, Loriann Hoff. *Surviving Separation and Divorce: A Woman's Guide to Making It Through the First Year.* Avon, MA: Adams Media, 2000.

Rufus, Anneli. *The Farewell Chronicles: How We Really Respond to Death.* New York: Marlowe & Company, 2005.

CHAPTER 3: *Are You Prepared for Your New Life? Your Life Alone?*

Brundige, Patsy and Pat Millican. *Hope For a Widow's Shattered World: Rebuilding Life out of the Ashes of Grief:* Lincoln, NE: iUniverse, Inc., 2003.

Felber, Marta. *Finding Your Way After Your Spouse Dies.* Notre Dame, IN: Ave Maria Press, 2000.

Feldon, Barbara. *Living Alone & Loving It: A Guide to Relishing the Solo Life.* New York: Simon & Schuster, 2002.

CHAPTER 4: *Have an Identity Crisis? Learn How to Get to Know Yourself*

Ackerman, Larry. *The Identity Code:The 8 Essential Questions for Finding Your Purpose and Place in the World.*
New York: Random House, 2005.

Tamura, Michael J. *You Are the Answer: Discovering and Fulfilling Your Soul's Purpose.*
Woodbury, MN: Llewellyn Publications, 2007.

Vanzant, Iyanla. *In the Meantime: Finding Yourself and the Love You Want.*
New York: Simon & Schuster, 1998.

CHAPTER 5: *A Cautionary Tale Go Slowly. Set Goals. Have a Plan*

CHAPTER 6: *Your Health and Exercise*

Fonda, Jane. *Prime Time: Love, Health, Sex, Fitness, Friendship, Spirit; Making the Most of All of Your Life.*
New York: Random House, 2012.

Sarasohn, Lisa. *The Woman's Belly Book: Finding Your True Center for More Energy, Confidence, and Pleasure.*
Novato, CA: New World Library, 2006.

CHAPTER 7: *Handling Stress: Create "My Place" for Meditation and Relaxation*

Beattie, Melody. *More Language of Letting Go: 366 New Daily Meditations* (Hazelden MeditationSeries). Center City, MN: Hazelden Publishing, 2000.

Ross, Steve. *Happy Yoga: 7 Reasons Why There's Nothing to Worry About.*
New York: Harper Collins, 2003.

Selby, John. *Quiet Your Mind: An Easy-to-Use Guide to Ending Chronic Worry and Negative Thoughts and Living a Calmer Life.*
Makawao, HI: Inner Ocean, 2004.

CHAPTER 8: *Be Kind to Me Day*

CHAPTER 9: *A Great New Look*

Hopkins, Christopher. *Staging Your Comeback: A Complete Beauty Revival for Women Over 45.*
Deerfield Beach, FL: Health Communications, Inc., 2008.

Johnson, Lois Joy; Sandy Linter, Bette Midler. *The Makeup Wakeup: Revitalizing Your Look at Any Age.*
Philadelphia: Running Press Book Publishers, 2011.

Shaevitz, Marjorie Hansen. *The Confident Woman: How to Charge and Recharge Your Life.*
New York, Three Rivers Press, 2001.

CHAPTER 10: *Face Your Sexuality Head On*

Banner, Lois W., *In Full Flower: Aging Women, Power, and Sexuality.*
New York, NY: Vintage, 1993.

Garity, Joan Terry, *The Sensuous Woman: The First HOW TO Book
for the Female Who Yeanrs to be All Woman.*
New York,: Dell, 1971.

Ogden, Gina. *The Heart & Soul of Sex: Making the Isis Connection.*
Boston, MA: Trumpeter Books, 2006.

CHAPTER 11: *Financial Security*

Coullahan, Joan and Sue van der Linden. *Financial Custody: You, Your Money, and Divorce.*
Indianapolis, IN: Alpha Books, 2002.

Dicks, James. *Operation Financial Freedom:
The Ultimate Plan to Build Wealth and Live the Life You Want.*
New York: McGraw-Hill, 2006.

Little, Ken. *Personal Finance at Your Fingertips.*
New York: Alpha Books, 2007.

CHAPTER 12: *Ready for Someone New? A Significant Other?*

Forleo, Marie. *Make Every Man Want You:
How to be So Irresistible You'll Barely Keep From Dating Yourself!*
New York: McGraw-Hill, 2008.

CHAPTER 13: *Looking for a New Type of Relationship?
A Woman Friend, Companion, or Lover, or a Male Confidant?*

Pimental-Habib, Richard L. *The Power of a Partner:
Creating and Maintaining Healthy Gay and Lesbian Relationships.*
Los Angeles: Alyson Books, 2002.

Berzon, Betty. *Permanent Partners:Building Gay and Lesbian Relationships that Last.*
New York, NY: Plume, 1990.

CHAPTER 14: *Consider a Younger Significant Other*

Emerson, David; and Jill Pitkeathley. *Age Gap Relationships:
The Attractions and Drawbacks of Choosing a Partner Much Older or Younger Than Yourself.*
New York: Thorsons, 1996.

CHAPTER 15: *Unconditional Love, a Pet*

Checchi, Mary Jane. *Are You the Pet for Me?: Choosing the Right Pet for Your Family.*
New York: St. Martin's Press, 1999.

Richard, James. *ASPCA Complete Guide to Cats:*
Everything You Need to Know About Choosing and Caring for Your Pet.
San Francisco: Chronicle Books, 1999.

Sikora Siino, Betsy. *Complete Idiot's Guide to Choosing a Pet.*
New York: Alpha Books, 1999.

Tortora, Daniel F. *The Right Dog for You: Choosing a Breed that Matches*
Your Personality, Family and Lifestyle.
New York: Touchstone, 1983.

CHAPTER 16: *Your Dream Job*

Hannon, Kerry. *What's Next? Follow Your Passion and Find Your Dream Job.*
San Francisco: Chronicle Books, 2010.

Kurth, Brian. *Test-Drive Your Dream Job:*
A Step-By-Step Guide to Finding and Creating the Work You Love.
New York: Business Plus, 2008.

McClure, Jason. *How to Find Your Dream Job and Make it a Reality:*
Solutions for a Meaningful and Rewarding Career.
Victoria, Canada: Trafford Publishing, 2003.

CHAPTER 17: *Positive Pursuits with a Purpose*

Brant, Keith. *Positive Pursuit: Principles for Personal and Spiritual Success.*
Bloomington, IN: Trafford Publishing, 2006.

Elgin, Duane. *Voluntary Simplicity: Toward a Way of Life that is*
Outwardly Simple, Inwardly Rich. Revised Edition.
New York: William Morrow, 1998.

Zandra, Dan. *Be the Difference.*
Compendium Publishing & Communications, 2004.
Newtown, PA

CHAPTER 18: *Pleasurable Pursuits*

Rand McNally. *Large Scale Road Atlas,*
United States, 2013. Chicago: Rand McNally, 2012.

Myers, David G. *The Pursuit of Happiness: Discovering the Pathway to Fulfillment,*
Well-Being, and Enduring Personal Joy.
New York: Avon Books, Inc., 1993.

Schaler, Karen. *Travel Therapy: Where Do You Need to Go?*
Berkeley, CA: Seal Press, 2009.

Schultz, Patricia. *1,000 Places to See Before you Die.*
2nd Ed. New York: Workman Publishing Company, 2011.

CHAPTER 19: *Pack Up and Move*

Allen, Paul. *The Truth About Moving Abroad and Whether It's Right for You:*
Should I Stay or Should I Go?
Great Britain: Summertime, 2010.

Ehrman, Mark. *Getting Out: Your Guide to Leaving America.*
Los Angeles: Process, 2006.

Kozik, Donna; Tara Maras. *29 Days to a Smooth Move.* 2nd Ed.
Lincoln, NE: iUniverse., 2005.

Poage, Martha. *The Moving Survival Guide: All You Need to Know to*
Make Your Move Go Smoothly.
Guilford, CT: Globe Pequot Press, 2004.

Savageau, David. *Places Rated Almanac: The Original Guide for*
Finding Your Best Places to Live in America.
Chicago: Independent Publishers Group, 2011.

Velazquez, Jodi. *Slick Move Guide. Secrets You Need to Know If You are Moving.*
Oakdale, PA: Knepper Press, 2007.